Atsushi Hayakawa

Circulation of Fire in the Veda

Nijmegen Buddhist and Asian Studies

edited by

Paul van der Velde und André van der Braak

Volume 2

LIT

Atsushi Hayakawa

Circulation of Fire in the Veda

LIT

This book is printed on acid-free paper.

Bibliographic information published by the Deutsche Nationalbibliothek
The Deutsche Nationalbibliothek lists this publication in the Deutsche Nationalbibliografie; detailed bibliographic data are available in the Internet at http://dnb.d-nb.de.

ISBN 978-3-643-90472-0

A catalogue record for this book is available from the British Library

Klosbachstr. 107
CH-8032 Zürich
Tel. +41 (0) 44-251 75 05
Fax +41 (0) 44-251 75 06
E-Mail: zuerich@lit-verlag.ch
http://www.lit-verlag.ch

LIT VERLAG Dr. W. Hopf
Berlin 2014
Fresnostr. 2
D-48159 Münster
Tel. +49 (0) 2 51-62 03 20
Fax +49 (0) 2 51-23 19 72
E-Mail: lit@lit-verlag.de
http://www.lit-verlag.de

Distribution:
In Germany: LIT Verlag Fresnostr. 2, D-48159 Münster
Tel. +49 (0) 2 51-620 32 22, Fax +49 (0) 2 51-922 60 99, E-mail: vertrieb@lit-verlag.de
In Austria: Medienlogistik Pichler-ÖBZ, e-mail: mlo@medien-logistik.at
In the UK: Global Book Marketing, e-mail: mo@centralbooks.com
In North America: International Specialized Book Services, e-mail: orders@isbs.com
e-books are available at www.litwebshop.de

Preface

The present work was started in 1994, but could not be finished until now due to various — essentially financial — problems. I am glad that I can now present the totality of my ideas on the development of the Vedic fire cult.

I would like to express my gratitude to my supervisors Prof. P.J.C.L. van der Velde and Dr. T.H. Quartier. Without their help I could not have finished this work.

I am also indebted to Prof. H.W. Bodewitz, under whose guidance I wrote most of the philological part, and to Prof. J.C. Heesterman, who helped me to start the research.

I would also like to mention the kind help of my friend, Etonian classicist Martyn Thirlway, who always encouraged me during these years and also corrected my English.

Almost half of the present work is based on my three articles published in *Asiatische Studien*. I would like to express my thanks to Prof. J. Bronkhorst and the editors of this journal for their kind permission to revise and republish these papers.

Chapter 1 “Three Steps to Heaven” was originally published in *Asiatische Studien* in 2000 under the same title. I have added some minor corrections to the original version.

Chapter 2 “Descent of Fire” consists of two sections. The section “Agni’s Birth in the Highest Heaven” is based on my publication in *Asiatische Studien* in 2001 under the same title. The section “Agni’s Landing” has been newly added for the present work.

Chapter 3 “Circulation of Fire” was written for this monograph.

Appendix “Mātariśvan, Heaven, Underworld” was published in *Asiatische Studien* in 2003 under the same title.

There are some prominent specialists who read the previously published constituents of this book and helped me to elaborate them. Among them, I especially thank Prof. Sh. Einoo, Prof. T. Gotō, Prof. B. Oguibénine, Prof. E. Pirart, and Prof. J.E.M Houben. I also thank Prof. H. Isoda, Drs. J. de Breet and the late Dr. L.A. van Dalen, who introduced me into the Indology, and Rev. T. Jinno and Prof. K. Miyazaki, who gave me constant moral support.

Last but not least, my gratitude goes to the three girls in my life, namely my wife Annick and our daughters Aska and Yoshino, who taught me the meaning of the vast region outside the Indology, which is called real life.

Leiden, December 2013 Atsushi Hayakawa

Table of Contents

Introduction: Rituals, Vedic Rituals, and Vedic Myths

The present study is primarily a philological study of the Vedic mythology, while it is also intended to be a contribution to the ritual studies. I would like to explain how these two aspects can be integrated into a single work, as described below.

Language Game

Language game, a concept introduced by Ludwig Wittgenstein, seems to me to be a good place to start our discussion. First I present an example of language game from my own experience and show why it can be our starting point.

When my nephew was almost two years old, I happened to have a chance to play with him. He was sitting in the room with some plastic stamps and a sheet of paper, and I saw one stamp with a circle on it and one with a triangle. I took a stamp and stamped a circle, saying "Maru!" (circle). My nephew immediately took another stamp and stamped a triangle, shouting "Sankaku!" (triangle). Now I stamped three times, shouting as loudly as he did, "Maru! Maru! Maru!" He also stamped three times, without lowering the tone, "Sankaku! Sankaku! Sankaku!" Again I stamped "Maru! Maru! Maru! Maru! Maru!" and he stamped again precisely five times, "Sankaku! Sankaku! Sankaku! Sankaku! Sankaku!" I then stopped stamping. My nephew also stopped.

When I started this game, I had not explained anything to him, I just stamped a circle. I did not even say that we were going to play a game. I stamped, and he answered it by stamping, and when he did it, a rule of the game was created between us. We continued to play, and the rule expanded further. I stamped three times without knowing how he would react, and he stamped as many times as I did without knowing why I stamped three times. In other words, no one defined the rule, and we didn't even know there was a rule. We just answered each other by stamping and shouting, and it gave our actions certain meanings.

Wittgenstein's starting point is the observation that the meaning of a sentence is the role it plays in its actual use. For example, a simple utterance "Coffee" can be an order in one situation, but it can be a description in another. Thus it can either be "Bring me a cup of coffee" or "This is coffee (and not tea)" according to the situation[1]. This might sound rather self-evident, but it means that the use of language is woven into the ac-

[1] PI 21: "Now what is the difference between the report or statement "Five slabs" and the order "Five slabs!"? — Well, it is the part which uttering these words plays in the language-game."

tions and the interactions of the people who communicate with each other, and that an spoken sentence cannot have a definite meaning outside the context of the interaction. Wittgenstein tried to demonstrate how meaning is generated in the interactive situations using the typical patterns of language use, which he called the language games.

Inasmuch as the meaning of a sentence is not based on a mental process or mental image separated from its actual use, the basis of communication must be linked to the institutions or conventions between the players in the language game. And this means that if someone consistently follows a different set of rules in a certain situation, the language game cannot take place[2]. This crucial condition to enable a language game is called "the agreement in the form of life"[3]. Suppose you are walking along a street in an unknown land. You see a place which looks very much like a coffee shop. You go into it, sit down and say "Coffee" to the waiter. The waiter immediately binds your hands behind you and sends you to a coffee plantation, where you are forced to work as a slave. It is obvious that we cannot communicate with such people, because we have different forms of life. Our language games are sustained by the facts that the coffee shop is not a slave hunting ground and that the waiter brings you a cup of coffee when you say the word "Coffee" to him. Further, Kikai (2003: 298ff), based on the study of M. Mizumoto, calls attention to Wittgenstein's term "surroundings" (*"Umgebung"*), which refers to a special environment created by the institutions. For example, money can only exist within the surroundings created by the monetary institution[4]. And the actions taken outside those surroundings do not constitute a language game, even if they are following the same logic[5].

---

[2] Kripke (1982: 95ff) gives a clear explanation as to this point.

[3] PI 240: "Disputes do not break out (among mathematicians, say) over the question whether a rule has been obeyed or not. People don't come to blows over it, for example. That is part of the framework on which the working of our language is based (for example, in giving descriptions)." PI 241: "'So you are saying that human agreement decides what is true and what is false?' — It is what human beings *say* that is true and false; and they agree in the *language* they use. That is not agreement in opinions but in form of life."

[4] This example is given by Wittgenstein himself in PI 584.

[5] Wittgenstein presents interesting examples of this point: PI 249 "Are we perhaps over-hasty in our assumption that the smile of an unweaned infant is not a pretence? — And on what experience is our assumption based? (Lying is a language-game that needs to be learned like any other one.)" PI 250 "Why can't a dog simulate pain? Is he too honest? Could one teach a dog to simulate pain? Perhaps it is possible to teach him to howl on particular occasions as if he were in pain, even when he is not. But the surroundings which are necessary for this behavior to be real simulation are missing."

The game with my nephew can be seen as a language game in which the rules of game are dynamically generated through the interaction of two players[6]. Our forms of life agreed, and the surroundings created in which we could play a language game. Using it we communicated with each other. And as a result, human relation was formed between the small child and myself.

Now, suppose we have decided to play the same game every day, but for some reasons we have decided to carry it out as a series of fixed rules for the participants *A* and *B*, as follows:

A stamps a circle while saying "Maru".
B stamps a triangle while saying "Sankaku".
A stamps three circles while saying "Maru" for each one.
B stamps three triangles while saying "Sankaku" for each one.
A stamps five circles while saying "Maru" for each one.
B stamps five triangles while saying "Sankaku" for each one.

When we carry this out as a procedure, we are confronted with a totally different situation: There is no interaction here, no direct communication between us. We act simultaneously, but in fact we follow the rules separately. We do not answer to each other by our actions anymore, we just play our own roles. In other words, we have no *surroundings* which should enable a language game, and therefore each rule does not work as a language game. We cannot make sure that our forms of life agree with each other. The only language game which can possibly be taking place here is "to execute the rules".

It is obvious that the above series of rules represent a simplified form of a certain type of ritual. I propose to call these kinds of executable rules which prescribe procedure "procedural rules", to distinguish them from the other types of rules, e.g. rules of game[7].

---

[6] Wittgenstein often takes chess as an example, and seldom mentions cases in which rules are generated. However PI 83: "And is there not also the case where we play and — make up the rules as we go along? And there is even one where we alter them — as we go along."

[7] Rules of game define basic entities of the game and control its flow, but you cannot execute these types of rules. I think it is worthwhile to mention here why I do not use the framework on rules presented by Searle (1969). Searle makes a distinction between two different sorts of rules, namely regulative and constitutive rules, and sketches the difference of these types as follows: "Regulative rules regulate a pre-existing activity, an activity whose existence is logically independent of the rules. Constitutive rules constitute (and also regulate) an activity the existence of which is logically dependent on the rules." Typical examples of constitutive rules are the rules of chess,

We have observed that the language game works differently when you execute a series of procedural rules. Or I can better say: execution of procedural rules is a language game in which the language game is restricted. This means that you create a space in which language games lose their effect. And, because almost everything in this human world consists of language games, it forms a discontinued island in the middle of the world. It is a sort of non-world. This might sound strange, but you can imagine the actual world, in which you work together with, show friendship to, or fight with people, and compare it with the situation in which all of these activities are substituted with procedural rules. Executing procedural rules never results in cooperation, friendship, fight or hatred. It creates a framed, qualitatively different space where nothing real may happen. And as long as language games are continuously going on, you can only get out of it when you play a language game within which language games do not take effect. Let us call this special space "the ritual space", because it typically happens in a ritual.

It is quite noteworthy that here we are in fact confronting the problem which Frits Staal presented as "the meaninglessness of ritual". Compare my observation above with that of Staal (1989: 132):

> What is essential in the ceremony[8] is the precise and faultless execution, in accordance with rules, of numerous rites and recitations. The result is important, but it has only ritual use and can only be reached in the ritually prescribed manner. I could not come in and assist in the proceedings by picking up the fire from the Old Altar and depositing it on the New. In fact, if I did such a horrible thing, the entire ceremony would be desecrated, interrupted, and expiation rites would have to be performed. Similar disasters

---

which create the actual possibility to play chess. For example, the rule "a checkmate is made when the king is attacked in such a way that no move will leave it unattacked" defines and enables the checkmate. An example of a regulative rule is "Take off your shoes at the entrance". In this case, the rule only regulates the manner of an existing activity, namely entering a house. Regulative rules typically take the imperative form "Do *X*" or "If *Y* do *X*", while constitutive rules often take the form "*X* counts as *Y*" or "*X* counts as *Y* in context *C*". The problem is: our rules appear regulative in form, but they must be constitutive according to the definition. Also, I have the strong impression that this distinction is not very meaningful in the context of rituals. Ritual rules are in principle constitutive in that the existence of the ritual is dependent on them. However, most of them are regulative at the same time in that they regulate an existing manner of actions.

[8] Staal is discussing the Vedic Agnipraṇayana "transporting the fire" here.

> would result if anyone used the sacred fire for any but a ritual purpose, e.g., to heat water for tea.
> Now contrast this with an ordinary activity. I am about to transport my suitcase from my house to the bus stop, which is about a mile away. There are no rules I have to follow, provided I obtain the desired effect. I may put my suitcase on a skate board. Or my brother may appear on a bicycle, and the two of us use this vehicle to transport my suitcase to its intended destination.

Although Staal does not connect the problem of ritual to that of a language game, he knows that the execution of rules leads to a completely different mode of human behavior. We tried to substantiate the border of ritual and non-ritual from the viewpoint of language game and communication, and have arrived at the path opened by Staal. In the next section we are going to examine his theory.

Meaning and Meaninglessness of Ritual

Staal (1989) is full of innovative ideas, but if we summarize them in one sentence, it will be as follows: Ritual is pure activity, without meaning or goal[9]. There are pros and cons, but an obvious advantage of this idea is that it can sweep away some apparently insoluble philosophical problems about rituals. For example, according to a typical functionalist theory, people invented ritual to maintain the solidarity of clan. On the other hand, intellectualists think that people invented ritual to explain things[10]. However, both types of theories have problems. That there is a connection between ritual and social organization does not yet mean that one was caused by the other. In the same way, the fact that a ritual presents explanation about the world does not yet mean that ritual was invented to explain it. But as long as you think that ritual has a certain meaning or function, you cannot exclude the intention from our scheme. And as long as you presuppose intention for ritual, you cannot eliminate the invention of ritual based on that intention. By denying the meaning and goal of ritual, we can eliminate these kinds of problems. Further, we know that the material which Staal is based on — the Vedic Agnicayana ritual — is extremely complicated, and that it is difficult to find any consistent meaning in it. Thus the motif with which he presented his theory is quite understandable. However, the grounds for his theory should in any case be examined.

Staal's theory not only clears up the theoretical perspective of ritual studies, but it also has a steady philosophical background and is rooted in

---

[9] Staal (1989) p.131.
[10] Like R. Horton.

the recent anthropological arguments concerning the nature of ritual. Catherine Bell (1997: 68ff) gives a clear overview of his position in human sciences. Here I present a short summary of her description in order to define a frame of reference for our discussion on the meaninglessness of ritual: John Austin first put forward the concept of the instrumentality of language. Austin (1962) noticed that some utterances are not descriptions of something, but can in themselves be regarded as actions. For example, when a person says "I christen this ship the Queen Elizabeth" the utterance is not a description of what he is doing, but the sentence is itself the action of naming a ship. Austin and his successor John Searle investigated various statements in our everyday life and established the theory of speech acts. This theory had a profound effect on ritual studies. Inasmuch as ritual utterances are speech acts, it is not sufficient to analyse their meanings. A group of theorists, represented by Edmund Leach, Stanley Tambiah and Maurice Bloch, who were opposed to the semantic school of Victor Turner and Clifford Geertz, began to pay attention to the syntactic patterns in rituals, which would act on the mind of the participants. Staal entered with this history as background. He made use of some concepts from Noam Chomsky's generative grammar and presented an image of ritual as rule-governed activity. However, a difference between language and ritual is that the latter has no intrinsic meaning, and he states that the proper object of ritual studies is the syntactic structure of ritual and not its meaning which in fact does not exist.

A quite interesting point of Bell's view is that it places Staal's theory in the line of Austin's works, while we rather see its essential connection to Wittgenstein. Staal (1989) mentions Austin as one of the sources of his inspiration. So this positioning seems to agree with his self-recognition. Another point is that there are actually two independent motifs in Staal's theory. That ritual has syntactic structure is not a logical consequence of the meaninglessness of ritual. Meaninglessness is also not a consequence of syntactic structure. Staal (1989) treats these motifs in an ingenious way. He presents the syntactical structure of ritual as the only legitimate object of the ritual studies by showing that the other candidate, the meaning of ritual, is absent.

Syntax of Ritual

Let us begin with the ritual syntax first. There are certain recursive patterns in Vedic rituals, and Staal proposes to use the term "syntax of ritual" to denote them. A simple example of such a pattern is given in Staal (1989: 87ff) as "$B \rightarrow ABA$", which means that the action B can be expanded by the action A so that two instances of A sandwich B. This pattern is recursively applicable. So for example, if you apply it five times, you will get "$A_1A_2A_3A_4A_5BA_5A_4A_3A_2A_1$"[11]. Staal gives several more examples of such patterns[12].

It *might* be possible to describe this system of embedding and transformation as ritual syntax. However, when we see his discussion against the background of the earlier discussion of Maurice Bloch and Stanley Tambiah, I am not really sure whether it is *proper* to do so. I will first present a short summary of their arguments below. Both works are quite comprehensive and contain a lot of important motifs about ritual, but here I mention only the points related to the ritualistic repetition.

Bloch (1974) starts from the presupposition that the propositional force of language is dependent on the syntactic freedom. So when the linguistic freedom is restricted, the propositional force of language is reduced. According to Bloch, ritual is a typical area where syntactic variation of language is restricted by the formalization of language[13]. And when the propositional force of language is reduced, communication is impoverished and as a result the performative force of language increases. In such a situation language is no longer used to report facts, but to influence people[14]. Based on this scheme, he gives an explanation as to the question why there are so many repetitions in ritual: inasmuch as there is no possibility to discuss propositional truth, repeating the same phrase is the only way to persuade people.

---

[11] The example from the Vedic Agnicayana ritual given by Staal (1989: 88) has a slightly asymmetrical form "$A_1A_2A_3A_4A_5BA_5A_3A_4A_2A_1$".

[12] See Staal (1989) chapter 11 "Embedding and Transformation" and chapter 16 "Music and Ritual".

[13] I cannot agree with Bloch on this point. That it has totally nothing to do with the freedom of syntax is obvious when we see the richness and the fertility of the Vedic language used in the ritual. As far as the grammatical system is concerned, we use much more impoverished language than the Vedic Indians did.

[14] Again, I cannot agree with Bloch on this point. He refers to Austin (1962) and uses the term "performative" to mean "to influence people". But every utterance of a sentence is in fact intended to influence people in one way or other. So if we use the term "performative" as Bloch does, any utterance is performative as long as something is meant. However, the verbal procedures in a ritual are embedded in rules, and they are just played, instead of providing meaning. So as a logical consequence, the sentences uttered in ritual cannot be performative. If you say to someone "bring water, please" outside ritual, it can be a "performative" utterance in which you ask him to bring a glass of water. However, if you say it inside the ritual space, the words should not have an effect on the people there. A participant may do it only if it is prescribed. Otherwise nothing should happen. See also Staal's discussion cited above.

Stanley Tambiah's work on the performativeness of ritual (1979) was seemingly written as a reaction to Bloch (1974). According to Tambiah, a ritual procedure can be associated with a certain object according to a conventional semantic rule, and at the same time with another object in a somewhat indexical way. And the latter typically represents the rank and privilege of participants. For example, the recitation of a sacred text can have a certain symbolical meaning, but at the same time the duration of the recitation can represent the social rank of the person for whom the ritual is carried out. The greater the scale of a ritual, the more there are redundant recitations[15].

When we see Staal's theory in this context, it is clear that he is giving yet another answer to the same problem: ritual action is repeated because the rule is recursively applicable. Staal's answer appears solid, because Vedic ritual does have built-in recursive rules. But in fact it only explains *how* repetition takes place, and still does not answer the question *why* it happens. Suppose you are a designer of Vedic ritual. You have a choice when writing a certain procedure: to define a single rule or to define a series of rules which are recursively constructed. You may choose the former or the latter, but if you choose the recursive structure, what is the reason for it? And when we return to the question "What is the necessity that causes the recursive rules to be chosen?", we see a clue to this problem in Tambiah's answer: From the viewpoint of our model, repetition of a certain procedure for a certain duration means that the ritual space continues precisely so long as the procedure is repeated. So, when for example a certain social rank demands a certain temporal duration of the ritual space, some of the procedures are repeated just to fill up the time. The royal topknot-cutting ritual, which Tambiah takes as example, and the Vedic Agnicayana of Staal are both rituals for people of power, who commit as much resources as they can to demonstrate their power. And, while it is quite easy to say "the ritual should continue for three days", it is rather difficult to invent new contents for it. So inventing repetition patterns which can be applied according to the demand of clients is a quite safe solution for such a situation.

When we think in the way mentioned above, we especially have a problem with the term "syntax" which Staal uses. Do the recursive patterns of Staal really deserve to be called syntax, if they are applied only to fill up time and express nothing at all? Syntax of a language produces a sentence and its meaning. In fact we cannot imagine a system of syntax without semantics. Staal presents music as an example of such a system[16], and indeed music conveys nothing which can be called meaning. Howev-

---

[15] Tambiah (1979) section "Variants of the Topknot-Cutting Ceremony in Thailand" (p.155ff).

[16] Staal (1989) chapter 16 "Music and Ritual".

er, it seems to me quite remarkable that the structure of music is never talked of in terms of "syntax" in the normal use of language, and according to me, the fact that it has no semantics is the reason for this. Both music and ritual have recursive patterns and they are applied to fill up a certain frame. But I am not keen on calling such systems of recursion "syntax". There is at least no necessity to use this term. I propose to call this type of recursive structure "involution patterns".

Meaninglessness in Animal Rituals

Staal apparently has strong grounds for the meaninglessness of rituals, which is the fact that animals have rituals[17]. Because the existence of symbolic systems has never been reported for animals, ritual certainly precedes symbolic system. However, his argument on animal rituals contains a fatal problem. The following text from Eibl-Eibesfeldt (1966: 475-476; referring to Lorenz 1963) is cited by Staal himself[18]:

> During the breeding season the male marine iguanas become territorial. They defend a small area of lava rock against other males, whilst females are allowed to stay. If a male rival approaches the territory, its owner displays. He opens his mouth, nods with the head and walks stiffleggedly up and down in front of the rival, showing his lateral aspect. The dorsal crest is erected and the gular regions extended. If the rival answers by the same display, fighting is initiated. The opponents rush at each other. But in spite of the biting intentions shown during the display they never bite each other, but instead lower their head and butt. The horn-like scales on the roof of the head interlock and the animals try to push the other away. This can continue for a while, with pauses in between, during which the opponents display frontally. The struggle ends when one of the rivals is pushed from the rock or when he gives up by assuming a submissive posture (lying flat on his belly). The winner then stops fighting and waits in threat display for the rival to leave. The fight is a highly ritualized tournament in the course of which the stronger wins, without hurting the loser.
>
> * * *
>
> Ritualized fighting is fairly widespread in animals that are capable of inflicting serious damage to the conspecific. Poisonous snakes never bite each other, but the rivals wrestle according to fixed

---

[17] See Staal (1989: 127).

[18] See Staal (1989: 435).

> rules. Cichilid fishes have developed various forms of mouthfighting and thus avoid mutual damage. In a number of species, e.g. in wolves, fighting starts as a damaging fight, but ends by a submissive posture of the loser, which inhibits further aggression.

The ritualized fighting of marine iguanas has a definite function in breeding. And far from being meaningless, it even conveys messages which they can never express outside the ritual: "Go away. This is my territory." There is no room for doubt that these types of messages are exchanged in these animal rituals, because otherwise a real fight would immediately take place. So I cannot help thinking that the rituals of these animals primarily serve as vehicle of meaning. Therefore, when we admit the continuity between animal rituals and human rituals, this will — quite contrary to Staal's intention — suggest that human rituals are also meaningful. And when we do not admit the continuity, this argument by Staal is not relevant to human rituals. In any case, the existence of meaningful animal rituals cannot be considered grounds for the meaninglessness of human rituals. So this discussion is just irrelevant.

Meaninglessness of Verbal Procedures of Ritual

Another important discussion from Staal dealing with the meaninglessness of ritual is his treatment of the verbal procedures in rituals. Here he follows two lines of strategy. First, he tries to demonstrate the meaninglessness of ritual by indicating the irrelevance of the verbal procedures in Vedic rituals[19]. Each action in Vedic ritual is in principle accompanied by a mantra[20], and so one would expect that there should be a correspondence between the action and the accompanying mantra, but in fact in most cases the mantra does not refer to the action. Indeed, if a totally irrelevant god is invoked, for example, at the lifting up of the dead body in the cremation ritual, you might think that the invocation has no meaning. However, this can never be a reason to conclude that verbal procedures are meaningless, because the simultaneous occurrence of a verbal procedure and a nonverbal procedure does not necessarily mean that the verbal procedure is an explanation of the nonverbal procedure. A verbal procedure does not have to be semantically dependent on a nonverbal procedure. So discordance between non-verbal and verbal procedures does not necessarily mean that the verbal procedures are meaningless.

---

[19] See Staal (1989) pp.195-196.

[20] ĀŚS 24.1.38, cited by Staal (1989: 193)

Staal's second strategy is to show their formal absurdities in concrete procedure of Vedic ritual[21], and he successfully presents an example of the Ṣoḍaśī Śastra, in which original verses are cut and pasted and intertwined to the point that they are completely meaningless. In the example given by Staal, a verse in anuṣṭubh meter (2×32 syllables) is fabricated from a gāyatrī verse (3×8 syllables) and a paṅkti verse (5×8 syllables), which means $2 \times 32 = 3 \times 8 + 5 \times 8$. The resulted verse is completely unintelligible. However, this does not happen everywhere in the Vedic ritual system, and as far as I see it is exceptional. Caland and Henry (1906) documents all the mantras used in the Agniṣṭoma, the basic form of the Soma rituals, but these mantras are in principle intelligible. So Staal's generalization is not justified, even on the level of the Vedic rituals.

Meaning

When we started this discussion, we agreed with Staal in our interpretation of the nature of the ritual rules. However, his grounds for defending the meaninglessness of ritual have turned out to be untenable. This does not yet mean that his main thesis — ritual is pure activity, without meaning or goal — is wrong, but we can no longer pursue his methodology, by which he tried to establish the grounds using the above discussion. Although I admit that the study of the involution patterns is quite important for the Vedic studies, it is certainly not the only legal target of ritual studies. It should not be called the study of ritual syntax either. To my regret, we have to find our own way to approach rituals.

Wittgenstein (1979: 12e) gives an interesting argument, which appears to be helpful for us:

> I read, amongst many similar examples, of a rain-king in Africa to whom the people appeal for rain *when the rainy season comes*. But surely this means that they do not actually think he can make rain, otherwise they would do it in the dry periods in which the land is "a parched and arid desert".

If this ritual was really intended as a rain-charm, they would carry it out in the dry season to make it rain. The fact that they do not do this means that they have no real intention to make it rain through the ritual. In other words, people do not carry out this ritual to achieve something. Although there is an objection to this argument by Ayer (1985: Chapter 7) from the standpoint of logical positivism, I believe that Wittgenstein is

[21] See Staal (1989) especially Chapter 18 "Ritual Context", (5) *indra juṣasva...*

right in principle. Many of us go to a temple once in a while. You pray there, while you have no intention to achieve something through your prayer. You pray just because it is a convention, and you know quite well that prayer does not make you a millionaire. Maybe Ayer did not have a habit of expressing his natural wishes towards himself in a conventional form, or maybe he never wished to become a millionaire. Wittgenstein (1979: 4e) says:

> Burning in effigy. Kissing the picture of a loved one. This is obviously *not* based on a belief that it will have a definite effect on the object which the picture represents. It aims at some satisfaction and it achieves it. Or rather, it does not *aim* at anything; we act in this way and then feel satisfied.
>
> * * *
>
> The description [*Darstellung*] of a wish is, *eo ipso*, the description of its fulfillment.
> And magic does give representation [*Darstellung*] to a wish; it expresses a wish.

The most important point of this argument is that in fact it grants no place to the function or the symbolism of ritual. However, he does not say that ritual has no meaning. When you throw a picture of someone you hate in the fire, the action does not aim at achieving anything in that you are not intending to accomplish anything with it, but you know the meaning of your behavior quite well. Just in the same way, people who carry out the "rain-charm" do not aim to achieve anything with it, but are giving expression to their rejoicing at the arrival of the rainy season. And when we see Staal's theory from this point, we understand what Staal did capture and what he possibly did not. He correctly understands that the symbolism of ritual is not directly connected to the meaning that the participants give to their experience. They can agree with each other, but they do not have to. However, he uses the same term "meaning" to denote these two types of meaning, and this is seemingly the reason why many people hesitate to accept his theory[22].

As we have already seen above, Staal's theory is generally understood as being in the context of Austin and Chomsky. However, the above discussion has shown another side of his theory. The best part of his theory

[22] Our discussion comes close to that of Oguibénine (1994) when he states: "Autrement dit, les significations, en effet, ne sont pas saisies uniquement selon ce que dénotent les signes du rituel, car elles se situent aussi bien à l'intérieur qu'à l'extérieur de l'ensemble signifiant qu'est le rite."

is in the context of Wittgenstein's thought, while his arguments that are inspired by Austin and Chomsky are untenable. Staal's theory is still brilliant, but its brilliance is not on the visible side of the street, but in the backyard. Our observation will be naturally understood when one goes back to the general character of Austin's and Wittgenstein's philosophies. What Austin tried to describe was how sentences function in ones life. Ritual without any meaning or function is in fact out of his range. On the other hand, according to Wittgenstein meaning is not something given. It only arises through ones practice based on the conventions. We all create social meanings with our actions, just as a football player gives a solution to various contexts within the game. And ritual is the place where it never happens. Obviously the meaninglessness of ritual as we understand it is much more accessible from Wittgenstein's position than from Austin's. I propose to recognise Staal as a successor of Wittgenstein and to accept his findings.

When we understand Staal's theory as essentially referring to the break between the symbolism of ritual and what the participants experience as the meaning of ritual, his theory is quite significant and his arrow hits the mark. However, it seems to cause another problem: if a ritual does not aim at anything and its content is not based on the intention of the participants, how can it survive for thousands of years? A clue to this problem was given by recent works on the relation between rituals and the obsessive-compulsive disorder (OCD). Although the similarity between the OCD and rituals had already been indicated by many scholars, Dulaney and Fiske (1994), cited by Boyer (2002), substantiated it with the results of neurological research. There is a certain cerebral region which concerns the planning and control of human actions. So, for example, when you are standing on a platform and a train has arrived, the relevant mental system handles different plans for actions, which can possibly include springing into the track. In normal cases, such a plan is rejected without causing a big impact. But in case of OCD patients, the relevant cerebral region is excessively activated and it causes a dramatic reaction, for example feeling acute terror and moving to the other end of the platform. The similarity between rituals and the OCD is especially visible in the cases concerned with hygiene. For example, a strong concern with purification appears both in rituals and in the OCD. Boyer (2002: Chapter 7) explains it with concepts from evolutionary psychology. The human brain has different modules to handle different problems. These modules were historically formed through the evolution process of mankind, and consciousness itself does not know what is actually going on within them. The infection system is one of such modules, and it protects you from various kinds of infections. A clear example of its working is given by Rozin (1976), and cited by Boyer (2002). When the examinee sees a cockroach in a glass, he will not like to drink water from the glass even after it is sterilized. According to Boyer, the infection system plays the main role in many cases of the OCD and rituals. So, for example, the purification of participants and the ritual enclosure implies the existence of infection, and the activated infection system handles the potential danger.

The idea that an invisible mental module is working behind rituals is plausible. And if this is the case, we now see a totally new landscape. It is no longer valid to talk about the origin and the continuance of rituals in terms of their functions. Of course rituals have social functions, but these might possibly have nothing to do with their origin. In that case, ritual just exists and continues to exist, driven by invisible mental processes[23].

---

[23] Although I am not in the position to start a new psychological discussion, I would like to indicate a point where our argument on rituals possibly encounters the forefront of psychologists. According to Tomasello (1999), the only major cognitive difference between human beings and other primates is that human beings understand others as subjects having intentions, while other primates do not. Chimpanzees are the most intelligent primates except for Homo sapiens. Although they can observe other chimpanzees' behaviour and learn from this, the way they learn is definitely different from ours. They understand the change of status before and after the action of another chimpanzee, or imdeed a human being to some extent, and they can emulate it, but they never understand the intention behind the behavior. For example, when a chimpanzee mother rolls a log over and catches insects under it, the child chimpanzee learns it, not by understanding the behavioral strategy of the mother, but by seeing the change of status caused by her action. So if you experimentally teach a chimpanzee and a two-year old human child to use a certain tool in an inefficient manner to reach a result, the human child reproduces the inefficient behavior of the instructor, while the chimpanzee does not try to reproduce the behavior, but the result. In other words, there is no essential difference between another chimpanzee and an inanimate object for the subjective world of a chimpanzee. Human children begin to understand other human beings as subjects having intentions when they are around 9 months old. For us, the interesting point of Tomasello's theory is that there is a striking similarity between rituals and the subjective world of the young babies he described. As we have seen, a ritual world is a place where procedural rules are executed without intention. People do not act based on intentions, but are just following rules. And imagine that you are standing in a ritual enclosure and watching people carrying out a ritual. You are looking at them without conceiving their intentions, just as a baby less than 9 months old does. My guess is that we are simulating the world of a baby by creating a ritual space, possibly to satisfy our legacy cognitive system of pre-9 months old and to keep it busy. So I suppose that we are basically in need of rituals somewhere in the depth of our hearts.

From Unintelligibility to Meaning

The above discussion suggests in any case that a phenomenon called ritual does not only contain the coding and decoding processes of messages. A large part of ritual is hidden, like an iceberg, under the water of unconsciousness, and it is driven by a hidden motive within ourselves. And when we look at rituals from the viewpoint of our consciousness, we should distinguish two levels of meaning: the symbolic meaning and the meaning which corresponds to the intention of the people carrying out the ritual. The significance of Staal's theory is that he indicated the break between these two levels of meaning.

It is not possible any longer for us to accept simplistic statements on the meaning of ritual. I quote here the words of Victor Turner (1972) as an example.

> The semantic structure of a dominant symbol may be compared with a ratchet wheel, each of whose teeth represents a conception or theme. The ritual context is like a pawl, which engages the notches. The point of engagement represents a meaning that is important in the particular situation. The wheel is the symbol's total meaning, and the complete range is only exposed when the whole cycle of rituals has been performed. Dominant symbols represent sets of fundamental themes. The symbol appears in many rituals, and its meanings are emphasized separately in many episodes. Since the settings in which the themes are ritually presentd vary, and since themes are linked in different combination in each setting, members of the culture who have been exposed to the entire ritual cycle gradually learn, through repettion, variation, and contrast of symbols and themes, what the values, rules, behavioral styles, and cognitive postulates of their culture are. Even more important, they learn in what cultural domains and with what intensity in each domain the themes should apply.

Like many other people, he believes that the symbolic meanings of ritual can directly touch the mind of the participants. Together with Staal, we now need to say a resolute "No" to this kind of bias. Turner's presupposition is that rituals are propaganda machines, but we have already seen that this is not the case. In the passage which follows the above, he argues the exegetical, operational, and positional dimensions of symbols. His analysis on this subject might be correct, but is completely irrelevant as long as it is not connected to the people's mind.

The meaning of a ritual is primarily what we can observe in it. Remember, for example, what you experienced at the funeral or the marriage of any of your family members. There happen really a lot of things, and most of them have nothing to do with the symbols of the ritual. I once attended a wedding where a person who had committed a serious sexual crime was invited as an important guest. Some people knew about this, but others did not. Those who knew about it were quite distressed and those who did not know did not understand why people behaved so strangely. I believe that many participants had the impression that something was wrong in this family, and if you ask me what the meaning of this commensuration ritual was, I cannot but say that it was this sad fact itself.

Some excellent works by anthropologists present examples of an approach to this type of the meaning of rituals. I would like to mention Geertz (1973: Chapter 15) here. In this impressive report about the Balinese cockfight, he describes how a cockfight can metaphorically depict the faces of the people who play it. What is at stake there is in fact not money, but status. And the greater the risk, the more significant the game becomes. Therefore, to participate in high level betting is to present one's self before the public. A cockfight is comparable to a duel, and it is a dramatization of people's concerns regarding status. It is interwoven in the Balinese social system, and reflects the network of social relationships. When the game starts, "death, masculinity, rage, pride, loss, beneficence, and chance" come to the fore in the form of the fighting cocks and in the tension of the betting, and it shows what people have in themselves in a clear and definite form. In other words, it is "a story they tell themselves about themselves".

The "meaning" which we see in this ritual is what the participants experience, and the formal structure of the cockfight itself does not seem to contain particular symbolical messages that express "a story they tell themselves about themselves". The cockfight begins to tell a story only when the betting has started, being embedded and entangled in the social structure and emotions of the participants. The "meaning" of the cockfight is revealed in the social behavior of people, while the cockfight itself is not intended to serve for anything, exactly in the same way as someone who prays definitely knows why he is praying, while the contents of the prayer are not intended to serve for anything.

Geertz threw a strong light on how society plays a ritual. However, quite disappointingly, this type of approach is difficult to adopt by those who study historic rituals, simply because the society which interacted with the ritual is not directly observable by us[24]. Actually the only thing left to us is the symbolic system of the ritual, of which the meaning is not relevant to the mind of the participants. Is it really meaningful to study the symbolic system of a ritual?

---

[24] This problem shadows Staal (1983) and all of his succeeding works.

As has already been mentioned, a Vedic ritual can be made infinitely more complicated by repetition and insertion. So the original procedure *B* could be embellished, thereby becoming $A_1A_2A_3A_4A_5BA_5A_4A_3A_2A_1$ for example, and this may mean that hundreds of irrelevant verbal and non-verbal procedures are inserted while *B* is executed. Moreover, the intention with which certain ritual procedures are designed is quickly forgotten, while the procedures themselves are often very precisely transmitted. As a result you may have a ritual lasting more than 10 days which is possibly meaningful, but is almost unintelligible for the participants. The Vedic Agnicayana is one of such rituals, and its overwhelming absurdity caused Staal to say that it is all meaningless. However, I would like to restart our discussion with the following question: Is intelligibility really essential to the production of meaning?

I would like to draw attention to the theoretical framework presented by Dan Sperber. Sperber (1996: 67) introduces the term "susceptibility": We, *Homo sapiens*, have a disposition to eat sweet foods. This tendency was developed during human evolution and clearly had an adaptive value in the severe environment in which our ancestors had to survive. However, the susceptibility to the overconsumption of sugar in our modern society is another result of the selection in the evolution. When we put this idea in the context of the human cognitive process, we can explain the origin of our mysterious ideas in terms of susceptibility: We have an ability to deal with information which we do not really understand. For example, I cannot follow the reasoning that justifies the formula "$e=mc^2$", but normally I put it into the formulation "$e=mc^2$ is valid", and treat the statement as a truth. This meta-representational ability has obviously an adaptive value, because without this ability we could not deal with the information which we do not understand. However, then, how about a statement like "The unconscious is structured like a language"?[25] When we put this statement in the formulation "'The unconscious is structured like a language' is valid" and treat it as a truth, the problem is to provide an interpretation for the statement. And the conceptual mysteries are developed in this way, by the susceptibility produced by the meta-representational ability. Here, we are already taking a step towards a religion.

I would like to take a simple example. Imagine that you are sitting with a patient suffering from Tourette's syndrome and you do not know it[26]. When he suddenly shouts "Testicles! Testicles! Testicles!", a certain bundle of associations concerning testicles will immediately arise in your mind. There is in fact no communication at all between you and him. His

[25] Sperber (1975) 4 "Symbolism and Knowledge". The cited sentence is a statement by Jacques Lacan.

[26] I have a mild form of Tourette's syndrome.

words just evoke associations. And you apparently have a good reason to believe that he wanted to say something about testicles. If you are a person who respects social norms, you might immediately call the police. In any case, when you confront such an unintelligible behavior, you try to understand his behavior to complete the image. Sperber (1996: 73) says:

> Evocation can be seen as a form of problem solving: the problem is to provide a more precise interpretation for some half-understood idea. This is done by searching encyclopaedic memory for assumptions and beliefs in the context of which the half-undersood idea makes sense.

And this seems to be what happens in your mind when Lacan says "The unconscious is structured like a language" or when I shout "Testicles! Testicles! Testicles!" However, the latter is not as famous as Lacan's statement, and Sperber further explains why this is so:

> The most evocative representations are those which, on the one hand, are closely related to the subject's other mental representations, and, on the other hand, can never be given a final interpretation. It is these *relevant mysteries*, as they could be described, which are culturally successful.

Many rituals are more or less unintelligible. Participants in such a ritual stand within a space where a lot of unintelligible actions take place. They could understand some part of verbal procedures, but ritual involution makes it impossible to reconstruct a consistent image. You might hear the names of gods and maybe could trace some cosmic motifs. However, the totality of the story is still covered by a thick mist. You know that you are in an extraordinary world governed by different orders from the actual world, and that something special is being told at that moment. Such a ritual appears as a riddle. The existence of an unknown part of the world is suggested, but you cannot experience it. The names of gods are mentioned, but you cannot make contact with them. The ritual asks you a question: What is this all about? And it leaves you alone in the ritual enclosure. The question lingers on in your mind and grows. Like every riddle, this riddle absorbs you and urges you to answer.

So what an unintelligible ritual presents is a question, and not an answer. The thicker the mist, the deeper the riddle. And the deeper the riddle, the stronger the urge to answer it. What matters in this case is not the intrinsic meaning, but the process in which the meaning is generated. In other words, a ritual asks you, "What is the meaning of this ritual?" and waits until you give an answer yourself. And when such "relevant mysteries" are presented, it is difficult for us to suppress our desire to give an explanation of them. The original intention with which the symbolic system of a ritual was constructed is in many cases more or less conjecturable. There might also be transmitted elucidations on the symbolic meaning of some procedures. The net of associations grows with such things as a core.

I think I need to mention Jean Baudrillard's theory about simulacra and simulation here. Although his discourses are not always intelligible for me, Baudrillard (1994) contains some important notions for us. According to him, simulation is as follows.

> Simulation is no longer that of a territory, a referential being, or a substance. It is the generation by models of a real without origin or reality: a hyperreal. The territory no longer precedes the map, nor does it survive it. It is nevertheless the map that precedes the territory — precession of simulacra — that engenders the territory and if one must return to the fable, today it is the territory whose shreds slowly rot across the extent of the map. It is the real, and not the map, whose vestiges persist here and there in the deserts that are no longer those of the Empire, but ours. *The desert of the real itself.*

A ritual presents us with a riddle, and we are urged to answer to the question, which actually has no answer. It is you that complete this simulation, and the completed simulation has neither origin nor reality. This seems to be a typical example of what Baudrillard called hyperreal, a map preceding the territory. A religious system is hyperreal, developed from the relevant mysteries. And rituals have a crucial position within the systems of religious simulation because of their unintelligibility. This seems to indicate two points: First, it is probably the reason why religion often appears as a system of waste. Secondly, the so-called postmodern has already existed for 3000 years.

Let us summarize our discussion. Ritual can be seen as a pure activity, when we leave out the invisible processes in our mind. The symbolic meaning of a ritual is not directly connected to the meaning or function of the ritual in the given society. However, it will not be deliberate enough if we assert that ritual is without meaning. Ritual can be unintelligible, but the very unintelligibility produces a lot of meanings. How could you call a ritual meaningless, when its simulacra cover up your whole world?

In the following section, I will outline how we approach Vedic rituals in the present work, based on our discussion so far.

Vedic Rituals and Myths

The classical Vedic rituals are described in Śrautasūtras, Gṛhyasūtras, and Pitṛmedhasūtras. The Śrautasūtras contain the descriptions of public rituals, and the Gṛhyasūtras those of domestic rituals. The Pitṛmedhasūtras are dedicated to the funeral ritual. Although we cannot establish the precise chronology of the Vedic literature, Renou and Filliozat (1947: 302) estimate that most of the sūtras were compiled between 400 B.C. and 200 B.C. These Sūtras are preceded by the Brāhmaṇas, which are elucidations of the rituals. The procedures described in the Brāhmaṇas agree with those of the Sūtras quite well. The Brāhmaṇas are further preceded by the Saṃhitās. Most parts of the Saṃhitās consist of verses, and the verses recited in the Vedic rituals are mostly taken from them. There are four classes of Saṃhitās: Rigveda, Atharvaveda, Yajurveda, and Sāmaveda. Each of the Brāhmaṇas and the Sūtras belongs to one of these classes. The oldest of the Saṃhitās is the Rigveda Saṃhitā. Oberlies (1998: 155) estimates the compilation date of its youngest hymns at around 1100 B.C.. The four classes of the literature correspond to the schools of the ritual officiants. The Rigveda belongs to the Hotṛ priests, who are specialized in reciting its verses, the Atharvaveda to the Brahman priests, who are supervisors concerned with the correct execution of the ritual procedures. The Yajurveda belongs to the Adhvaryu priests, who execute the most nonverbal procedures, and the Sāmaveda to the Udgātṛ priests, who sing the Sāmavedic songs. Some of the rituals, like Agniṣṭoma and Agnihotra, are already mentioned in the Rigveda Saṃhitā.

Although the Rigveda in wider sense includes the Rigvedic Brāhmaṇas and Sūtras, it is a convention to denote the Rigveda Saṃhitā with the term "Rigveda".

Here I present a description of a simple procedure from the Baudhāyana Pitṛmedhasūtra as an example. This is a procedure to bring the sacrificial fire and the deceased sacrificer to the site of cremation. The English translation below is taken from the Śrautakośa.

BPS 1.3.11ff	The fires should be collected (into vessels) and carried. Or the fires should be consigned (into the kindling woods), or they should be carried with the dead body held amidst them. The dead body should then be lifted up. The adhvaryu should follow the dead body, being lifted up, with *pūṣā tve 'taś cyāvayatu...* After one-third of the road (to the cremation-ground) has been traversed, the dead body should be put down. One should immolate one of the young goats without using a weapon. If the goats have not become available, the adhvaryu should stir up (and

> take out) the cooked rice (out of the cooking vessel) with the corn-stirring stick. If there is only one vessel of cooked rice, he should stir up one-third of the cooked rice with the corn-stirring stick, gather clods of earth, and cast away that portion of cooked rice upon those clods. The wives, led by the youngest and with their hair ruffled, should go round the dead body by the left, three times, fanning it with the hems of their garments. So also should the kinsmen and (other) ladies do. After having tied up the hair, the wives should again go round, three times, in the reverse direction.

The verse "*pūṣā tve 'taś cyāvayatu...*" recited here is from the Taittirīya Āraṇyaka, but it is originally from the Rigveda[27]. The Rigveda Saṃhitā consists of 1028 hymns, 10462 verses, and this point forms a unique characteristic of the Vedic rituals. While most of the rituals documented by anthropologists do not have a repository of parallel passages for the verbal procedures, we have the whole Vedic corps. We certainly know that the god Pūṣan ("*pūṣā*"), who is mentioned in the verse, has about a hundred occurrences in the Rigveda Saṃhitā. If you would like to know why a certain god is mentioned in a certain context of ritual, you can check all the relevant passages from the Rigveda and other Vedic literature. A verse mentioning Pūṣan contains an implicit reference to the whole mythology around this god. — You could compare it with a monad which represents the whole universe, or with a jewel of Indra's net which reflects all the other jewels. — And this is the very point where a philological study of the Vedic mythology can be a study of ritual at the same time. By the study of the mythological context, we could trace the lines of possible associations of the Vedic Indians. And when it is seen in the context of the ritual, it is a study of the connotation of a certain point of the ritual, which can be a starting point for the development of an interpretation. This might be comparable to drawing a tangent line to a curve.

[27] The Taittirīya Āraṇyaka and the Baudhāyana Pitṛmedhasūtra belong to a Yajurvedic school. The relevant part of the Taittirīya Āraṇyaka is a Rigvedic mantra collection for the people of the Yajurvedic school.

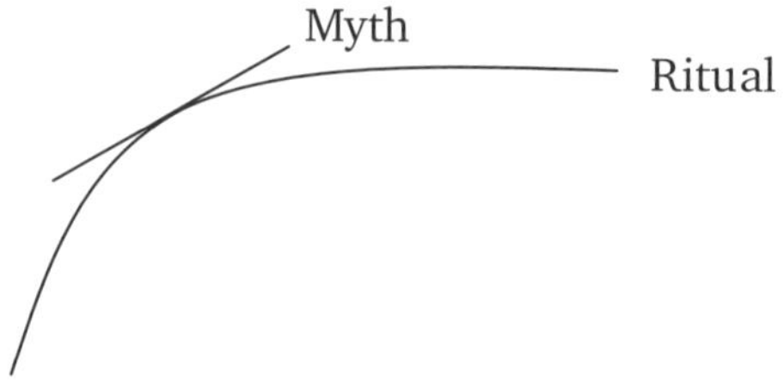

The Brāhmaṇa literature represents the interpretation of the "relevant mysteries" more or less in development. As Staal (1989: 117ff) indicates, the Brāhmanas are not reliable sources from which to get information about facts, but it was probably not intended by the compilers of these documents to present facts about the Vedic religion. So we could better use the information from the Brāhmaṇas as the material to follow the development of the simulation, as shown in the next image[28].

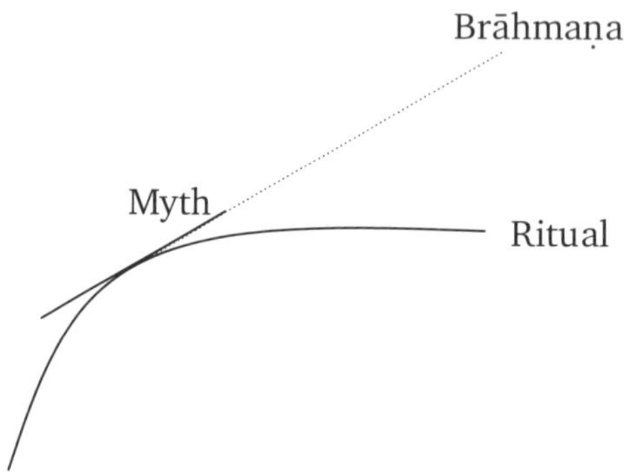

The present study deals with two series of mantras. The one is the verses from the Taittirīya Āraṇyaka 6.1.4, of which the most verses are taken from the Rigvedic hymn 10.16. In the ritual context, these verses are recited at the moment when the body of the dead sacrificer is set on fire. The other series is the Rigvedic hymn 3.3. These verses are recited in the Agniṣṭoma ritual, in the procedure called The Third Soma Pressing. Although these mantras are in themselves quite interesting for mythological study, my interest is the point where the two lines of the interpretation cross each other.

[28] The studies on the meanings of the Vedic rituals and their procedures according to the Brāhmaṇas like Einoo (1985) can be located on this line.

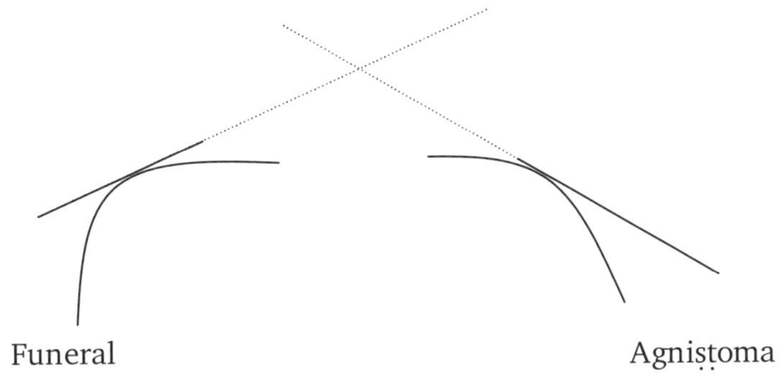

This is the point where I expect that a developed simulation appears, which is derived from two simulacra. An important theme of the present work is to indicate the location where it is documented in the Brāhmaṇa literature, and to demonstrate how it is connected with the two series of verses recited in the rituals.

We will deal with the Vedic funeral ritual in Chapter 1, and the Third Soma Pressing of the Agniṣṭoma in Chapter 2. In Chapter 3, we will deal with the esoteric doctrine called *Pañcāgnividyā*, which I expect to be the crossing point of the two tangents. The philological introduction to each theme and the reference to earlier studies will be provided in the chapters where they are discussed.

In short, the central aim of the present work is to observe how "relevant mysteries" grow up to become a fully developed simulation and emerge as an archaic doctrine at the beginning of the history of the Indian philosophy.

Chapter 1: Three Steps To Heaven

A question arises from the five mantras of TĀ 6.1.4[29], which are recited at the moment of cremation according to Baudhāyana Pitṛmedhasūtra 1.8. In these mantras, Agni, Agni Jātavedas, and Agni Vaiśvānara are invoked in that order. The question is: Why are these three types of Agni invoked in this ritual procedure? In other words, do they have different functions which are particular to each of them? Four of the relevant verses of TĀ 6.1.4 are taken from the Rigveda. Let us first look at earlier studies concerning Vaiśvānara and Jātavedas in the Rigveda to find a good starting point for our study.

Earlier Studies on Vaiśvānara and Jātavedas

The best point to begin the discussions about the Rigvedic Vaiśvānara is the following verse, which contains typical features of Vaiśvānara:

RV 1.59.2	Agni is the head of heaven, the navel of earth. And he became the aratí of heaven and earth. The gods created you as such a god. O Vaiśvānara, [you are] the light for the Aryan[30].

Pāda a: Oldenberg (1894) does not discuss Vaiśvānara in detail[31]. Macdonell (1897: 99) indicates that there was a difference of opinion about Vaiśvānara's location even in the time of Yāska[32]. Hillebrandt (1899: 114ff) identifies "the head of heaven" in the above verse with the sun and "the navel of earth" with the sacrificial fire. Keith (1925: 164) largely follows Hillebrandt and identifies Vaiśvānara with the sun and the sacrificial fire. The identification of Vaiśvānara with the sun is plausible in itself, as well as its identification with the sacrificial fire. But a problem arises in any case as a result of these identifications: How can Agni

[29] I follow the Ānandāśrama and Bibliotheca Indica editions in the numbering of the passages. In the Mysore edition, these verses are contained in 4.1.4. For the text, see the section "To Heaven" of this chapter.

[30] *mūrdhā́ divó nā́bhir agníḥ pṛthivyā́ áthābhavad aratī́ ródasyoḥ / táṃ tvā devā́so 'janayanta deváṃ vaíśvānara jyótir íd ā́ryāya //*

[31] He discusses Agni as the sacrificial fire (p.102ff) and Agni as the sun (p.108ff), but does not metnion Vaiśvānara there. Oldenberg Noten and Oldenberg SBE do not give important information on this Pāda.

[32] "Yāska in commenting on the epithet states (Nir. 7, 23), that ancient ritualists (*yājñikāḥ*) took Agni Vaiśvānara to be the sun, while Śākapūṇi considered him to be this Agni."

Vaiśvānara be the heavenly sun and the earthly sacrificial fire[33]? Findly (1982) collected the Rigvedic material about Vaiśvānara widely, and tried to present its comprehensive image. But as to the duality of Vaiśvānara, she leaves the problem unsolved[34].

Pāda b: The word *aratí* is translated as "Diener, Gehülfe, Verwalter, Ordner, administer" in PW, "der das Opfer zurichtet, zu stande bringt" by Grassmann, and "Lenker, Wagenlenker" by Geldner. While PW and Grassmann do not appear to help us, Geldner's interpretation is significant. Although later works such as Thieme (1949) and Findly (1982) seem not to have noticed it, by translating *aratí* as "Lenker", the heavenly Vaiśvānara and the earthly Vaiśvānara can be connected with each other through a mobile messenger. However, as Thieme (1949: 26) indicates, there are no good etymological grounds for *aratí* "Lenker"[35]. Thieme himself interpreted *aratí* as "Speichenkranz", which does not help us to understand Vaiśvānara's duality. Thieme's discussion will be examined later. Findly (1982) translates *aratí* consistently as "ministrant", which seems to have been taken from PW.[36]

Pāda d: Findly (1982: 15ff) indicates Vaiśvānara's aspect as the "conquering fire".

As to the name *vaiśvānará*, we will discuss it later at the end of the section "Three Steps" of this chapter. Relevant studies will also be mentioned there.

As to Jātavedas, we have a relatively small amount of secondary literature. Most of the earlier studies are concerned with the etymology of the name *jātávedas*. Findly (1981) presented the first comprehensive description of Jātavedas. She indicated three aspects of the Rigvedic Jātavedas: "the unbroken presence at the ritual", "the keeper of the family" and "the presence at the cremation ritual". Among these aspects, the last one seems to be important for us. She argues: "Unlike any other aspect of Agni, Jātavedas is consistently associated with the fire which burns corpses, which carries the dead to Yama's kingdom, and which offers

---

[33] Hillebrandt (1899: 115) says, "wir haben also einen V. im Himmel, einen auf Erden. So erklärt es sich, dass Nir. VII, 23 nach den Yājñika's Vaiśvānara die Sonne, nach Śākapūṇi aber "dieser Agni" ist." This indeed explains the difference of opinion in Nirukta, but of course it does not explain the duality of Vaiśvānara.

[34] Findly (1982: 10) "Rising up as the most visible luminary in the sky, Vaiśvānara must be worshipped as prominent among the gods. But remaining as he does on earth, Agni the fire is bound to his priestly function to serve these same gods as well."

[35] Mayrhofer's dictionary does not even mention "Lenker".

[36] Witzel and Gotō (2007) translate this word "Speichenschaft". This seems to be oriented to the same direction as the result of our discussion.

oblations to the ancestors." Jātavedas is invoked eight times in the Rigvedic funeral verses 10.15 and 16, and among them 10.16.1, 2, 4 and 5 mention the conveying of a corpse. It might be correct that Jātavedas has this function, but I would like to determine the function of Jātavedas in a more general form with more extensive material, so that we can understand the function of corpse-conveying as part of a more general function.

The above summary of earlier studies brings us to our starting points: 1) The problem of Vaiśvānara's duality, which Geldner attempted to solve through the interpretation of *aratí*. Are there any other solutions possible for its etymology? 2) The forms and functions of Vaiśvānara and Jātavedas: can they be more clearly described?

Material and Method

I define the Vaiśvānara verses as the verses in which Agni Vaiśvānara (or Vaiśvānara) is mentioned, not as the verses which are contained in the hymns dedicated to Agni Vaiśvānara. This definition is justified because the hymns which are said to belong to Vaiśvānara contain many verses that mention Agni, Agni Jātavedas, or some other manifestations. In other words, I only use the material which definitely belongs to Vaiśvānara. In earlier studies, the material was not defined explicitly[37].

The Rigvedic Vaiśvānara verses, which we obtain through this definition, are the following verses: RV 1.59.1; 1.59.2; 1.59.3; 1.59.4; 1.59.5; 1.59.6; 1.59.7; 1.98.1; 1.98.2; 1.98.3; 3.2.1; 3.2.11; 3.2.12; 3.3.1; 3.3.5; 3.3.10; 3.3.11; 3.26.1; 3.26.2; 3.26.3; 4.5.1; 4.5.2; 5.27.1; 5.27.2; 5.51.13; 5.60.8; 6.7.1; 6.7.2; 6.7.3; 6.7.4; 6.7.5; 6.7.6; 6.7.7; 6.8.1; 6.8.2; 6.8.3; 6.8.4; 6.8.6; 6.8.7; 6.9.1; 6.9.7; 7.5.1; 7.5.2; 7.5.3; 7.5.4; 7.5.5; 7.5.8; 7.5.9; 7.6.6; 7.6.7; 7.13.1; 7.13.2; 7.13.3; 7.49.4; 8.30.4; 9.61.16; 10.45.12; 10.88.12; 10.88.13; 10.88.14.

The method of definition of the Jātavedas verses is the same as outlined for the Vaiśvānara verses: The verses in which Agni Jātavedas (or Jātavedas) is mentioned. As far as I could collect, the Rigveda contains the following Jātavedas verses: RV 1.44.1; 1.44.4; 1.45.3; 1.50.1; 1.59.5; 1.77.5; 1.78.1; 1.79.4; 1.94.1; 1.99.1; 1.127.1; 2.2.1; 2.2.12; 2.4.1; 3.1.20; 3.1.21; 3.2.8; 3.3.8; 3.5.4; 3.6.6; 3.10.3; 3.11.4; 3.11.8; 3.15.4; 3.17.2; 3.17.3; 3.17.4; 3.20.3; 3.21.1; 3.22.1; 3.23.1; 3.25.5; 3.26.7; 3.28.1; 3.28.4; 3.29.2; 3.29.4; 4.1.20; 4.3.8; 4.5.11; 4.5.12; 4.12.1; 4.14.1; 4.58.8; 5.4.4; 5.4.9; 5.4.10; 5.4.11; 5.5.1; 5.9.1; 5.22.2; 5.26.7; 5.43.10; 6.4.2; 6.5.3; 6.8.1; 6.10.1; 6.12.4; 6.15.7; 6.15.13; 6.16.29;

[37] Findley (1982) seems to have defined the material in a different way. Some Rigvedic verses which she cites, such as 3.2.13-14, 10.88.1-11, 7.6.1-5, are not relevant material according to our definition.

6.16.30; 6.16.36; 6.16.42; 6.48.1; 7.2.7; 7.3.8; 7.5.7; 7.5.8; 7.9.4; 7.9.6; 7.12.2; 7.13.2; 7.14.1; 7.17.3; 7.17.4; 7.104.14; 8.11.3; 8.11.4; 8.11.5; 8.23.1; 8.23.17; 8.23.22; 8.43.2; 8.43.6; 8.43.23; 8.71.7; 8.71.11; 8.74.3; 8.74.5; 9.67.27; 10.4.7; 10.6.5; 10.8.5; 10.15.12; 10.15.13; 10.16.1; 10.16.2; 10.16.4; 10.16.5; 10.16.9; 10.16.10; 10.45.1; 10.51.1; 10.51.3; 10.51.7; 10.61.14; 10.69.8; 10.69.9; 10.83.2; 10.87.2; 10.87.5; 10.87.6; 10.87.7; 10.87.11; 10.88.4; 10.88.5; 10.91.12; 10.110.1; 10.115.6; 10.140.3; 10.150.3; 10.176.2; 10.188.1; 10.188.2; 10.188.3.

In 1.59.5, 6.8.1, 7.5.8 and 7.13.2, Vaiśvānara and Jātavedas are mentioned in the same verse. These require a separate discussion.

A Rigvedic god can be regarded as the sum of the attributes which are described and are attributed to him in the Rigveda. We can regard a god as a class, and his attributes as its elements. The attributes which are only contained in the class Vaiśvānara and not in the class Jātavedas are the attributes of Vaiśvānara. In the same way, the attributes which are only contained in the class Jātavedas and not in the class Vaiśvānara are the attributes of Jātavedas.

An ideal process would be as follows: First we extract the descriptions of Agni Vaiśvānara and Agni Jātavedas from the Rigveda. Then we obtain two classes of attributes, namely the class Vaiśvānara (V) and the class Jātavedas (J)[38].

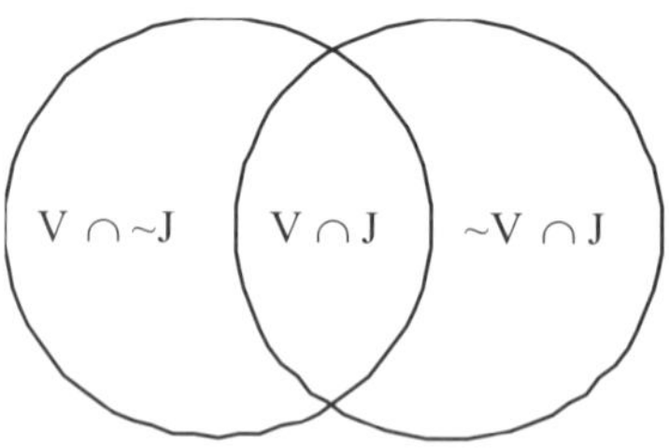

Vaiśvānara Jātavedas

If a certain attribute belongs to Agni in general and not in particular to the manifestations, then it must appear in both V and J. Therefore, if we restrict our domain of discourse to the classes Agni, Vaiśvānara, and Jātavedas[39], the class of the attributes which belong to Agni in general is

[38] The diagram below looks like a Venn diagram. In fact, I am abusing a Venn diagram, which represents the relationship between classes and their elements, to represent the relationship between entities and their attributes.

[39] I restrict our domain of discourse to keep our discussion simple. As a result, the terms "the attributes which are particular to Vaiśvānara/Jātavedas" and "Agni in general" are used in an approximate sense in this study. Precisely spoken (i.e. if we set our domain of discourse to "all the manifestations of

defined as the intersection of V and J, namely $V \cap J$. The class of the attributes which are particular to Vaiśvānara is $V \cap \sim J$. And the class of the attributes which are particular to Jātavedas is $\sim V \cap J$. If $V \cap \sim J = \sim V \cap J = \varnothing$, it means that there is only a nominal difference between Vaiśvānara, Jātavedas, and Agni[40].

The present chapter consists of two sections: In the section "Three Steps", the meaning of the word *aratí* will be examined first, and subsequently the forms and functions of Vaiśvānara and Jātavedas will be studied. The section "To Heaven" analyses the functions of Agni Vaiśvānara and Agni Jātavedas in the concrete context of the Vedic cremation ritual.

Three Steps

Aratí

As was already mentioned, Thieme (1949) gives the translation "Speichenkranz" for *arati*, which is also adopted by Mayrhofer. Now we should re-examine his discussion. Let us start with the following verse:

RV 6.3.5 — Like a shooter who is about to shoot, he puts on [the arrow]. He sharpens his flame just like an iron blade. The *aratí* of light[41] which has a bright course[42] is just like a bird sitting on a tree, which flutters quickly[43].

Agni"), the attributes which belong to $V \cap \sim J$ are not the attributes which are owned exclusively by Vaiśvānara, because there is a possibility that he shares the attributes with some other manifestations of Agni. In that case, "Agni in general" is the intersection of all the manifestation classes. Although I think the restriction to Agni, Vaiśvānara and Jātavedas is practically enough for our purpose, a study of other manifestations could calibrate the result of the present study.

40 Gonda (1959: 256) suspects that the instances of Jātavedas "may also to a certain extent be explained from metrical considerations". If he is right, there must only be nominal difference between Agni and Jātavedas.

41 Geldner: "der Lenker der Nacht" (He follows Ludwig's "der Bote der Nacht"). Mayrhofer: "leichtes Gleiten, Salbe, Schminke; lichte Farbe, Licht, Strahl; dunkle Farbe, Dunkel, letster Teil der Nacht". I take it "light", because *aratí* is said to have "a bright course" here.

42 Geldner: "von wunderbarer Schnelligkeit", however Mayrhofer (under *DHRAJ*): "mit glänzender Bahn".

43 *sá íd ásteva práti dhād asiṣyáñ chíśīta téjó 'yaso ná dhā́rām / citrádhrajatir aratír yó aktór vér ná druṣádvā raghupátmajaṃhāḥ //*

Aratí looks like “a bird sitting on a tree, which flutters quickly”. A “Speichenkranz” never looks like such a thing. Although Thieme (1949: 30) mentions this verse, he does not fully discuss it. In the following verses, *Aratí* is put down (*ni-ā-īr*) somewhere:

RV 2.2.3 — The gods have put down the marvellous *aratí* of heaven and earth on the bottom of the air. [They have put down] the brightly shining Agni who is to be known as a chariot, who is to be praised among the settlements like Mitra[44].

RV 10.3.7 — Let you bring the greatness hither for us. Let you put yourself down as *aratí* of the two young ones, [namely] heaven and earth. May swift, impetuous Agni come hither with the swift, impetuous horses[45].

Thieme identifies “the bottom of the air” in 2.2.3 with earth[46], which seems correct. He argues these verses in connection with Geldner’s interpretation “Lenker”: “*aratí* ist mehrfach, geradezu typisch, Objekt van *ny èrire* (1.128.8, 2.2.3), *nyerirè* (4.1.1, 8.19.21), das Geldner sicherlich richtig als Perfekt von *ni* + *ar* erklärt (anm. zu 4.1.1b), aber kaum treffend mit “haben bestellt als” übersetzt. “Sie haben eingefügt” führt viel eher auf einen Teil des Wagens als den Lenker als Objekt[47].” However, “the ‘Speichenkranz’ which is put down on earth” can only mean a broken wheel. In any case, something is wrong with this interpretation.

The etymological ground of Thieme's discussion is the interpretation of the suffix *-ti* as a collective sense. Although this might be possible, it is not the only possible interpretation. Liebert (1949: 178), who collected the instances of the suffix *-ti* from a wide range of material, takes *aratí* as denominative. He derives *aratí* from **ara* (“rechte, passende Art” < *áram*), and translates *aratí* “einer der die rechte, passende Art weiss, einer der das richtige Ritual kennt”. Liebert’s explanation does not fit the context of the above instances either, because a “ritual-knower” does not look like a bird on a tree. However, it leads us to the third possibility,

---

[44] *táṃ devā́ budhné rájasaḥ sudáṃsasaṃ diváspṛthivyór aratíṃ ny èrire / rátham iva védyaṃ śukráśocịsam agním mitráṃ ná kṣitíṣu praśáṃsyam //*

[45] *sá ā́ vakṣi máhi na ā́ ca satsi divásprthivyór aratír yuvatyóḥ / agníḥ sutúkaḥ sutúkebhir áśvai rábhasvadbhī rábhasvām̐ éhá gamyāḥ //*

[46] “Ihn (Agni), den sehr wunderkräftigen, haben die Himmlischen am Boden des Luftraums (= auf der Erde) als den Speichenkranz von Himmel und Erde eingefügt.” (p.30)

[47] Thieme (1949: 27). RV 10.3.7 is referred to in p.31, but not fully discussed.

which is mentioned neither by Thieme nor by Liebert: *Aratí* can also be derived from *ará* "spoke" as denominative.

AIG II,2 p639-640 mentions the following instances of the denominative *–ti*[48]: *pattí* (pedestrian) < *pad* (foot), *addhātí* (sage) < *addhā́* (truly), and *vṛkáti* (murderer) < *vṛ́ka* (wolf). Semantically this formation can be understood as the addition of "-man" in English. So, "foot-man" is a pedestrian, "truth-man" is a sage, and "wolf-man" is a murderer. Therefore, if we derive *aratí* from *ará* "spoke", it means "spoke-man", or a spoke as a god. And when we think of *aratí* as such, we can explain the above instances of *aratí*: *Aratí* is the spoke-god which supports the movement of the sun. When it stands upright, it looks like "a bird sitting on a tree" (RV 6.3.5), because in the Vedic mythology the sun is a great bird[49]. This interpretation also fits the context of RV 2.2.3 and 10.3.7 better. These verses clearly show a scene in which the gods fix the bottom end of the spoke-god on earth. The reason why the *aratí* is called "the *aratí* of heaven and earth" in these verses is also clear: The spoke-god extends from earth to heaven and combines them with each other.

The above RV 2.2.3 contains a comparison of Agni with a chariot. RV 10.3.7 mentions "swift, impetuous horses". Agni is often compared with a chariot, and it is one of the most important grounds for Thieme's interpretation. However, the verses cited by Thieme do not always support his interpretation. A good example is the interpretation of *dadṛśānápavi* "whose felloe has become visible" in the following verse[50]:

RV 10.3.6 — The hissing noises of him, when his felloe has become visible, [namely] when he gapes, sound forth. The most heavenly, far-reaching[51] *aratí* shines forth with the ancient, brilliant, harnessed horses[52].

Thieme explains: "Dem Dichter stellen sich die Flammen als schnaubende Rosse am Wagen, die vom Feuerschein umgebenen Flammen als die von der Radschiene umschlossenen Speichen eines Wagenrades dar." However, he is making a logical mistake here. He himself claims that *aratí* is a feminine

[48] AiG itself classifies *aratí* in "Anscheinend weder deverbal noch denominativ".

[49] Cf. Macdonell (1897) p.31.

[50] Thieme (1949: 32): "Es ertönt sein Ungestüm, wenn er durch seine Gespanne schnaubt, wenn seine Radschiene sichtbar wird, wenn er, der erste der Himmlischen, wachsend nach allen Seiten hin leuchtet als Speichenkranz (Wagen) durch seine alten, hellen, singenden [Speichen]."

[51] *víbhvan* Mayrhofer (under *BHAV*): "weitreichend".

[52] *asyá śuṣmāso dadṛśānápaver jéhamānasya svanayan niyúdbhiḥ pratnébhir yó rúśadbhir devátamo ví rébhadbhir aratír bhā́ti víbhvā //*

noun[53]. The genitives in 10.3.4 *asyá yā́māso bṛható ná vagnū́n índhānā agnéḥ sákhyuḥ śivásya,* 10.3.5 *svanā́ ná yásya bhā́māsaḥ pávante rócamānasya bṛhatáḥ sudívaḥ* and 10.3.6 should be taken as Sūrya as Geldner notes in 10.3.4 "*asyá*, des Sūrya", and not as *aratí*. The above verse depicts the rising sun ("when his felloes have become visible") and the spoke-god, which instantly extends itself from the rising sun to the sacrificial fire (or, from the sacrificial fire to the sun). "The harnessed horses" (*niyúdbhih*), which are also mentioned in 10.3.7 as *sutúkebhir áśvaiḥ*, is a figurative expression of the rays. The Vedic poets compared the extraordinary speed of the extending spoke-god with the horses, because they knew nothing faster than them. RV 2.4.2 *aratír jīrā́śvaḥ* "*aratí*, which has a quick horse" is based on this association. The "extending *aratí*" can also be seen in RV 6.15.4d *havyavā́ham aratíṃ devám ṛñjase* "I extend the god *aratí*, the conveyor of the oblation".

Thieme translates RV 6.12.3ab *téjiṣṭhā yásyāratír vanerā́ṭ todó ádhvan ná vṛdhasānó adyaut* "Der im Holz herrschende (Agni) ist erstrahlt, größer werdend wie ein Wagenfahrer auf der Straße (der immer näher kommt), er, dessen Speichenkranz sehr glühend ist." (p.29). Based on this verse, he claims that *aratí* is a feminine noun. However, even if RV 2.4.2 *devā́nām agnír aratír jīrā́śvaḥ* could be explained as assimilation to the gender of the qualifying noun, this verse cannot be decisive grounds on which to determine the gender of *aratí*, because *téjiṣṭhā* can also be the instrumental of *téjiṣṭha* (neut/masc)[54]. Moreover, Thieme's translation does not explain to us why *aratí* is like "a charioteer on the way". My translation is:

RV 6.12.3ab	[Agni], ruling in the wood, whose *aratí* grows with the most brilliant [horse] like a charioteer on the way, has shone.

Aratí extends quickly, like a chariot running in full speed with an extremely fast horse. The charioteer of such a chariot looks growing on the way, if you look at him from his destination, namely the sacrificial enclosure where the poet is standing.

The follwing verse seems to show an interesting problem of Thieme's chariot:

RV 8.19.1	The gods have caused the god *aratí* to run. They (priests) have offered the oblation to the gods[55].

---

[53] Thieme (1949: 32). However, RV 2.4.2d *devā́nām agnír aratír jīrā́śvaḥ* makes it less plausible.

[54] Grassmann also takes it as the instrumental.

[55] *devā́so devám aratíṃ dadhanvire devatrā́ havyám óhire //*

Thieme's translation of this particular verse seems acceptable (p.31): "Den Himmlischen (Agni) haben die Himmlischen als *aratí* laufen lassen, zu den Himmlischen haben sie [durch Agni] die Opferspeise gefahren." He argues: "Natürlich ist hier in dichterischer Ausdrucksweise ... mit "Speichenschaft" das ganze Rad oder der ganze Wagen gemeint." But the problem of Thieme's chariot is that its "Speichenkranz" is fixed on earth and in heaven. Therefore, it runs nowhere[56].

RV 4.38.4 has been translated in various ways. Thieme translates Pāda d "[der dahinläuft] ... schneller als die Speichenschaft (schneller als die Speichen sich drehen können)". Geldner: "Der im Kämpfen bis an die Wagendeche reichende (Beute) errafft, der als bester Gewinner hervorgeht, wenn er auf Rinder auszieht, seine Vorzüge offenbarend, die weisen Worte verstehend, seinen Lenker noch übertreffend, mehr als Āyu zu erreichen vermag." Renou EVP: "Lui qui, raflant les butins dans les combats, avance, gagnant (des richesses), allant (à la quête) de vaches, (ce cheval) aux marques bien-apparentes, attentif aux répartitions-rituelles, (qui est allé) au delà de l'emblème (solaire, qui) a en(touré de sollicitude) l'ouvrage de l'Āyu.":

RV 4.38.4 [The horse] which plunders booties at battle fields, which, as the best gainer approaching cows, foaming at the mouth [57] and observing the distribution, runs through *aratí* around the waters[58] of Āyu[59].

As far as the following two verses are concerned, Thieme's interpretation "Speichenkranz" does not cause a serious problem:

RV 10.3.2 When he approaches this black [night] with the pretended form, generating the maiden, [namely] the

---

[56] *Dadhanvire* is interpreted in a causative sense by Thieme, Geldner and Grassman "cause to run". But it could also be interpreted in a non-causative sense "run", taking the accusative as the object. In this case, the translation of the verse will be "The gods have run to the god *aratí*." See Gotō (1987: 178 note 309): "Selten mit Akk.: zum Haus (*kṣáyam*) IX 97,26, zum Kuh- und Roßbesitz (*gómat ... áśvavat*) IX 105,4 (möglicherweise Inhaltsakk.), zu Indra (von Agni) III 53,4; einmal mit Lok. (*Māṃścatvé ... sárasi*) IX 97,52; manchmal mit Dat. ('für jn.' bzw. finaler Dat.)".

[57] Mayrhofer (under *ṛjīka-*): "an dem der Schaum hervortritt".

[58] I take *ā́pas* as the accusative. The horse runs through the cosmic spoke and approaches the heavenly waters.

[59] *yáḥ smārundhānó gádhyā samátsu sánutaraś cárati góṣu gáchan / āvírṛjīko vidáthā nicíkyat tiró aratím páry ā́pa āyóḥ //*

	child of the great father, the *aratí* of heaven shines with Vasus, supporting the upward light of the sun[60].
RV 5.2.1	The young mother holds the covered baby secretly, and she does not give it to the father. People do not see ahead its not-changing face which is put on *aratí*[61].

Both of these verses are concerned with the break of dawn[62]. It might be possible to take the *aratí* of 10.3.2 and 5.2.1 as the morning sun with radiance. However, no other instance of *aratí*, which we have seen above, can be translated “Speichenkranz”. If we take *aratí* in these verses as the spoke-god, we can explain the Pādas cd of these verses as follows: At the break of dawn, the spoke-god forms a straight line towards the east, which runs on the surface of the earth. The morning sun, which is put on the tip of the spoke-god (5.2.1), shines upwards (10.3.2).

RV 1.59.2 *aratī́ ródasyoḥ* and 10.3.7 *diváspṛthivyór aratír yuvatyóḥ* have already been discussed. Similar instance is RV 7.5.1 *divó aratáye pṛthivyā́ḥ* “for the *aratí* of heaven and earth”. This is most naturally interpreted as “the spoke combining heaven and earth”.

While the interpretations “Speichenkranz” and “spoke-god” are primarily concerned with the spatial form of *aratí*, Liebert’s “ritual-knower” does not give a concrete visual image of *aratí*. Just because of it, this interpretation does not cause a problem in the contexts presented above. However, it also gives no clear vision of *aratí* as “spoke-god” does. In any case, it cannot explain why *aratí* grows like a charioteer on the way (RV 6.12.3), why it is said to support the upward light of the sun (RV 10.3.2), or why it is put down on the bottom of the air (RV 2.2.3)

On the etymological level, *aratí* can be taken as “Speichenkranz”, “ritual-knower”, or “spoke-god”. However, the above contextual study shows that the only possible interpretation is that of “spoke-god”. Let us go further and see what role the “spoke-god” plays in the mythological structure of Agni.

---

[60] *kṛṣṇā́ṃ yád énīm abhí várpasā bhū́j janáyan yóṣām bṛhatáḥ pitúr jā́m / ūrdhvám bhānúṃ sū́ryasya stabhāyán divó vásubhir aratír ví bhāti //*

[61] *kumārám mātā́ yuvatíḥ sámubdhaṃ gúhā bibharti ná dadāti pitré / ánīkam asya ná mináj jánāsaḥ puráḥ paśyanti níhitam arataú //*

[62] 10.3.2b “maiden”, “the child of the great father” is Uṣas. As to 5.2.1, Thieme (1949: 29) translates: “Die junge Mutter (= die Nacht) trägt den Knaben (= die Sonne) eingewickelt im Geheimen: nicht gibt sie ihn dem Vater (zur Anerkennung) Sein [die Satzungen] nicht täuschendes Gesicht (die stets pünktlich wiedererscheinende Sonnenscheibe) sehen die Völker vorn (im Osten) hineingesetzt in einen Speichenkranz.”

The Spatial Descriptions of Vaiśvānara and Jātavedas

In Brāhmaṇas we very often observe a threefold structure of the world[63]. It can be formulated as follows.

location	*the form of fire*
Heaven	Sūrya
Antarikṣa	Vāyu
Earth	Agni

Bṛhaddevatā[64] shows a slightly different structure.

location	*the form of fire*
Heaven	Agni Vaiśvānara
Antarikṣa	Agni Jātavedas
Earth	Agni

Here Agni Vaiśvānara and Agni Jātavedas appear instead of Sūrya and Vāyu, respectively. But as far as I know, this structure has not been positively attested to in the Vedic texts. Although Bṛhaddevetā does not belong to the Vedic corpus, and so we cannot conclude that this structure exists in the Vedic mythology based only on this passage, there might be a possibility that it contains some truth. So we will pay special attention to the spatial division of Vaiśvānara and Jātavedas.

As has already been seen, Vaiśvānara is identified with the sacrificial fire ("the navel of earth") and the sun ("the head of heaven").

RV 1.59.1 O Agni, other fires are only your branches. All the immortals rejoice at you. O Vaiśvānara, you are *the navel of the settlements*. You hold the people like a supporting pillar[65].

RV 1.59.2 Agni is *the head of heaven, the navel of earth*. And he became the spoke-god of heaven and earth. The gods

[63] E.g. TS 5.6.7, ŚB 6.1.2.10, etc. It is also said in the ŚB that Agni is threefold (ŚB 6.7.3.16, etc), and that Agni, Vāyu, Āditya are all the light of the world (ŚB 6.3.3.16). Cf. also Macdonell (1897) p93-94.

[64] 1.95-96 in Tokunaga's text, which correspond to Macdonell's 1.99-100.

[65] *vayā́ íd agne agnáyas te anyé tvé víśve amṛ́tā mādayante / vaíśvānara nā́bhir asi kṣitīnā́ṃ sthū́ṇeva jánām̐ upamíd yayantha //*

created you as such a god. O Vaiśvānara, [you are] the light for the Aryan[66].

The following verses describe his periodical ascent, which can be interpreted as that of the sun.

RV 3.2.12 — *Vaiśvānara has ascended heaven* as in the ancient time. Being honoured by good hymns, he [ascends] the top of heaven. Producing the wealth for people as before, the watchful one goes round the same course[67].

The following verses describe Vaiśvānara as the morning sun.

RV 10.88.12 — The gods created for all the people as *the banner of days* Agni Vaiśvānara, who, *coming with the light, extended the shining Uṣases* and also *covers up the darkness*[68].

RV 6.9.1 — The night and the day, [namely] two sides, rotate with [magical] knowledge. Vaiśvānara, being born, *overpowered the darkness with light*, just like a king[69].

The "celestial body", which is identified with Vaiśvānara, can also be interpreted as the sun.

RV 10.88.13 — The seers and the gods who are worthy of sacrifice, created Agni Vaiśvānara, who is not subject to old age, the ancient, unaltering, *moving celestial body*, the strong, high superintendent of the spirit[70].

Some verses mention the omnipresence of Vaiśvānara with his light. This can also be understood as an aspect of a solar deity.

---

[66] *mūrdhā́ divó nā́bhir agníḥ pṛthivyā́ áthābhavad aratī́ ródasyoḥ / táṃ tvā devā́so 'janayanta deváṃ vaíśvānara jyótir íd ā́ryāya //*

[67] *vaiśvānaráḥ pratnáthā nā́kam ā́ruhad divás pṛṣṭhám bhándamānaḥ sumánmabhiḥ / sá pūrvaváj janáyañ jantáve dhánaṃ samānám ájmam páry eti jā́gṛviḥ //*

[68] *víśvasmā agním bhúvanāya devā́ vaiśvānaráṃ ketúm áhnām akṛṇvan / ā́ yás tatā́noṣáso vibhātī́r ápo ūrṇoti támo arcíṣā yán //*

[69] *áhaś ca kṛṣṇám áhar árjunaṃ ca ví vartete rájasī vedyā́bhiḥ / vaiśvānaró jā́yamāno ná rā́jā́vātiraj jyótiṣāgnís támāṃsi //*

[70] *vaiśvānaráṃ kaváyo yajñíyāso 'gníṃ devā́ ajanayann ajuryám / nákṣatram pratnám áminac cariṣṇú yakṣásyā́dhyakṣaṃ taviṣám bṛhántam //*

RV 7.5.4 O Agni Vaiśvānara, the threefold world, heaven and earth follow your law. *You have spread over Heaven and Earth with your light, [namely] the perpetual, flaming glow*[71].

As was already seen above, Vaiśvānara is also described as a spoke-god.

RV 7.5.1 Bring praise to strong Agni, [namely] *the spoke-god of heaven and earth*, [namely] Vaiśvānara, who was brought up in the lap of all the immortals by the watchful ones[72].

RV 6.7.1 The gods generate Vaiśvānara, [namely] the Agni who is born regularly, the head of heaven, *the spoke-god of earth*, the seer, the universal king, the guest of the people, the drinking-vessel at the mouth[73].

The following Vaiśvānara verses contain some ambiguous expressions: RV 3.26.1 mentions *svarvíd* as an attribute of Vaiśvānara. Geldner translates it "Sonnenfinder" and notes "er bringt durch seine Helle die Sonne, d.h. Licht auf Erden". However, if his note represents his intention, PW and Grassmann "Licht, Glück, u.s.w. verschaffend" seems to me less misleading. Geldner translates *yatate* in RV 1.98.1 *vaiśvānaró yatate sū́ryeṇa* "wetteifelt". However, Gotō (1987: 254) and Mayrhofer: "in fester Weise eine Stellung einnehmen".

We have seen the spatial descriptions of Vaiśvānara[74]. Earlier studies, which translate *aratí* as "Speichenkranz" or "Lenker", could not reconstruct the form of Vaiśvānara as a unity and they left it divided in heaven and on earth. But now, through the new interpretation "spoke-god", we can present a more consistent form: The rotation of the sun is supported by the spoke, and "the navel of earth" functions as a pivot.

---

[71] *táva tridhā́tu pṛthivī́ utá dyaúr vaíśvānara vratám agne sacanta / tvám bhāsā́ ródasī ā́ tatanthā́jasreṇa śocíṣā śóśucānaḥ //*

[72] *prā́gnáye taváse bharadhvaṃ gíraṃ divó aratáye pṛthivyā́ḥ / yó víśveṣām amṛ́tānām upásthe vaiśvānaró vāvṛdhé jāgṛvádbhiḥ //*

[73] *mūrdhā́naṃ divó aratím pṛthivyā́ vaiśvānarám ṛtá ā́ jātám agním / kavíṃ samrā́jam átithiṃ jánānām āsánn ā́ pā́traṃ janayanta devā́ḥ //*

[74] Apart from these verses, there are some Vaiśvānara verses which describe the entering of Agni into the plants. Cf. RV 1.98.2, (and maybe also) 7.49.4. But the myth of entering into plants is not particular to Vaiśvānara. Cf. RV 10.51.3 (Jātavedas verse).

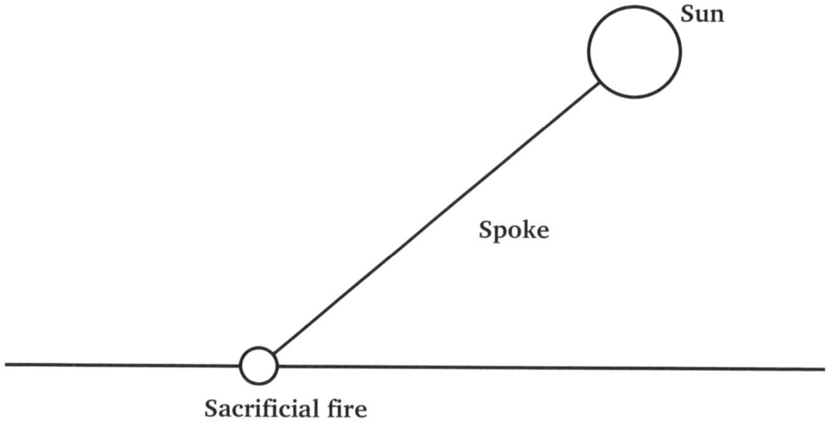

The spatial descriptions of Jātavedas are rather scarce, but in the following verse Jātavedas is put on "the place of libation".

RV 3.29.4 — *We put you on the footprint of the libation,* [namely] on the navel of earth, o Agni Jātavedas, to convey the oblation[75].

"The footprint of libation (= the navel of earth)" must be the sacrificial fire. And we should remember that the bottom of Vaiśvānara was also called the navel of earth. So here Jātavedas is spatially identified with the sacrificial fire[76]. Jātavedas is identified with the spoke-god in the following verse.

RV 3.17.4 — O Jātavedas, praising brilliant, beautiful Agni, we honour you, who are to be invoked. The gods made you the messenger, *the spoke-god,* the conveyor of the oblation, the navel of the immortality[77].

---

[75] *íḷāyās tvā padé vayáṃ nā́bhā pṛthivyā́ ádhi / jā́tavedo ní dhīmahy ágne havyā́ya vóḷhave //*

[76] Some other facts support this identification. First, the word "kindled" often attributed to Jātavedas: *índhāna* (being kindled inexhaustibly) RV 10.45.1, *sámiddha* (being kindled) 10.87.2, 10.110.1, 3.5.4, 6.15.7. *samidhāná* (flaming) 2.2.1, 7.9.4. *súsamiddha* (well-kindled) 5.5.1. Secondly, in the funeral verses the epithet *kravyā́d* is used to denote Jātavedas. (10.16.9 and 10.16.10) Thirdly, Jātavedas is once said to be "domestic (*dámya*)" in 3.2.8. He is also said to be "of Vadhryaśva (*vā́dhryaśva*)" in 10.69.9.

[77] *agníṃ sudītíṃ sudṛ́śaṃ gṛṇánto namasyā́mas tvéḍyaṃ jātavedaḥ / tvā́ṃ dūtám aratíṃ havyavā́haṃ devā́ akṛṇvann amṛ́tasya nā́bhim //*

The following Jātavedas verses contain some ambiguous expressions: RV 5.4.4b *yátamāno raśmíbhiḥ sū́ryasya* "occupying his place with the rays of the sun" does not identify Jātavedas with the sun. See Pāda d: *ā́ ca devā́n havirádyāya vakṣi* "And bring the gods for the oblation-eating". Here, Jātavedas brings the gods from heaven to earth, accompanied with the sunshine. RV 10.61.14 *bhárgo ha nā́motá yásya devā́ḥ svàr ṇá yé triṣadhasthé niṣedúḥ* "His name is Glare, to which the gods also [belong], who put [him] down on the threefold seat like the sun" is not an identification, but a comparison. One might interpret Jātavedas in the following verse as the rising sun: RV 10.88.5 *yáj jātavedo bhúvanasya mūrdhánn átiṣṭho agne sahá rocanéna / táṃ tvāhema matíbhir gīrbhír ukthaíḥ sá yajñíyo abhavo rodasiprā́ḥ //* "O Agni Jātavedas, when you stood on the head of the earth with the light, we have impelled you with the hymns, the songs of praise, and the Ukthas. You, being worthy of sacrifice, become the filler of the world." But "the head of the earth (*bhúvanasya mūrdhán*)" corresponds with "the head of the heaven". Therefore I would interpret it as the sacrificial fire on the fire altar. In 10.88.6, "the head of the earth" seems to be the sacrificial fire: *mūrdhā́ bhuvó bhavati náktam agnís* "At night Agni becomes the head of the earth." RV 2.2.1 contains the word *svàrṇara*. The meaning of this word is not clear. Mayrhofer quotes Renou EVP: "mot obscur et peut-être volontairement ésotérique" (Renou EVP 7 [1960] 43 [mit Lit]).–Der etymologischen Auswertung eines solchen Wortes sind Grenzen gesetzt."

Now we should look at the above figure again. Spatially, Vaiśvānara consists of the three parts: the sun, the spoke, and the sacrificial fire. But the spoke and the sacrificial fire are also identified with Jātavedas. And also, while Vaiśvānara is often identified with the sun, we see no identification of Jātavedas with the sun.

Therefore we should conclude as follows: The sun belongs to the own part of Vaiśvānara ($V \cap {\sim}J$). The sacrificial fire and the spoke, the common parts of Vaiśvānara and Jātavedas ($V \cap J$) belong to Agni in general. As to the spatial form, Jātavedas does not have a particular attribute (${\sim}V \cap J = \emptyset$).

Functions of Vaiśvānara and Jātavedas

Jātavedas appears in the Rigveda first and foremost as a conveyor. He brings gods, oblations, and other objects.

RV 1.44.1 — O immortal Agni, [bring] the shining, glittering gift of Uṣases. O Jātavedas, let you *bring the gods* who awake with the dawn to the pious one today[78].

RV 3.6.6 — Or put under the yoke of the regular order with the straps [a pair of] maned red [horses] whose surface is brilliant with ghee. And, o god, *carry all the gods*. O Jātavedas, carry out good sacrifices[79].

RV 5.4.4 — O Agni, being in accordance with the libation, let you enjoy. Occupying his place by means of the rays of the sun, o Jātavedas, enjoy our fire-wood. *Bring the gods hither* for eating the oblations[80].

RV 10.110.1 — Today being kindled in the house of a man, as a god you sacrifice for the gods, o Jātavedas. And, o Mitramahas[81], being wise, *bring [them] hither*. You are messenger, seer, wise one[82].

RV 10.150.3 — I praise you, [namely] Jātavedas, who bestows every treasure, with the hymn. O Agni, *bring the gods* who are fond of observance[83] hither for us. For the favour [bring] those who are fond of observance[84].

RV 3.11.4 — The gods made Agni Jātavedas, who is famous of old as the son of strength, *a conveyor*[85].

---

[78] *ágne vívasvad uṣásaś citráṃ rā́dho amartya / ā́ dāśúṣe jātavedo vahā tvám adyā́ devā́m̐ uṣarbúdhaḥ //*

[79] *ṛtásya vā keśínā yogyā́bhir ghṛtasnúvā róhitā dhurí dhiṣva / áthā́ vaha devā́n deva víśvān svadhvarā́ kṛṇuhi jātavedaḥ //*

[80] *juṣásvāgna íḷayā sajóṣā yátamāno raśmíbhiḥ sū́ryasya / juṣásva naḥ samídhaṃ jātaveda ā́ ca devā́n havirádyāya vakṣi //*

[81] The meaning of this word is not clear, but we can regard it as an epithet for Agni.

[82] *sámiddho adyá mánuṣo duroṇé devó devā́n yajasi jātavedaḥ / ā́ ca váha mitramahaś cikitvā́n tvám dūtáḥ kavír asi prácetāḥ //*

[83] The meaning of *priyávrata* is not clear. Geldner: "liebwaltend", PW: "erwünschtes Gesetz habend oder Gehorsam liebend", Grassmann: "liebe Gesetze habend".

[84] *tvā́m u jātávedasaṃ viśvávāraṃ gṛṇe dhiyā́ / ágne devā́m̐ ā́ vaha naḥ priyávratān mṛḷīkā́ya priyávratān //*

[85] *agníṃ sūnúṃ sánaśrutaṃ sáhaso jātávedasam / váhniṃ devā́ akṛṇvata //*

RV 3.29.4 We put you on the place of the libation, [namely] on the navel of earth, o Agni Jātavedas, *to convey the oblation*[86].

RV 5.9.1 The mortals invoke you, the god, with oblations, o Agni. I think you are Jātavedas. *Carry the oblations* one after another[87].

RV 5.26.7 Put down Agni Jātavedas, [namely] *the conveyor of the oblations*, the youngest one, the divine Ṛtvij[88].

RV 7.17.3 O Agni, *go with the oblation* and sacrifice for the gods. O Jātavedas, carry out good sacrifice[89].

RV 8.74.3 [I praise] wonderful Jātavedas, *who sends to heaven the oblations* which are lifted up with the divine service[90].

RV 10.15.12 O Agni Jātavedas, being invoked, *you have brought the oblations* after making them fragrant. You have given them over to the fathers with the refreshment[91]. They ate it. O god, eat the offered oblations[92].

RV 10.16.9 I send the flesh-eating Agni forward. Carrying impurity, let him go to the subjects of Yama. Here, let this other Jātavedas, the wise one, *bring the oblation to the gods*[93].

RV 10.16.10 For the sacrifice of the fathers, I carry the flesh-eating old Agni, who has entered into your house while seeing

[86] *ī́ḷāyās tvā padé vayáṃ nā́bhā pṛthivyā́ ádhi / jā́tavedo ní dhīmahy ágne havyā́ya vóḷhave //*

[87] *tvā́m agne havíṣmanto devám mártāsa īḷate / mányе tvā jātávedasaṃ sá havyā́ vakṣy ānuṣák //*

[88] *ny àgníṃ jātávedasaṃ hotravā́haṃ yáviṣṭhyam / dádhātā devám ṛtvíjam //*

[89] *ágne vīhí havíṣā yákṣi devā́n svadhvarā́ kṛṇuhi jātavedaḥ //*

[90] *pányāṃsaṃ jātávedasaṃ yó devátāty údyatā / havyā́ny aírayat diví //*

[91] *Svadhā́* seems to mean refreshment in the context of the funeral cult.

[92] *tvám agna īḷitó jātavedó 'vāḍ ḍhavyā́ni surabhī́ṇi kṛtvī́ / prā́dāḥ pitṛ́bhyaḥ svadháyā té akṣann addhí tváṃ deva práyatā havī́ṃṣi //*

[93] *kravyā́dam agním prá hiṇomi dūráṃ yamárājño gachatu ripravāháḥ / ihaívā́yám ítaro jātávedā devébhyo havyáṃ vahatu prajānán //*

	this other Jātavedas. *He will drive the Gharma* to the highest seat[94].
RV 10.51.7	We make your life ageless, so that you, who are harnessed, would not be injured, o Jātavedas. O well-produced one, being gracious, *you will bring the share of the oblation* to the gods[95].
RV 10.176.2	Offer the divine hymn to the god Jātavedas. *Let him bring our oblations* one after another[96].
RV 10.188.3	Let him invigorate our sacrifice with the lights of Jātavedas, which are *the conveyors of the oblations* to the gods[97].
RV 1.99.1	We press Soma for Jātavedas. He will burn down the wealth of the malevolent one. *He will bring us over all difficulties*. Just like a boat [brings us over] the river, Agni [brings us over] difficulties[98].
RV 5.4.9	O Jātavedas, *convey us across all the dangers and difficulties*, just as the boat [conveys across] the river. O Agni, being praised with praise just like by Atri, be protector of our body[99].
RV 5.43.10	O Jātavedas, being invoked, *carry all the Maruts* hither with names and forms. O Maruts, let all of you go to the sacrifice, the songs of praise, and the excellent admiration of the singer, all with protection[100].

---

[94] *yó agníḥ kravyā́t pravivéśa vo gṛhám imám páśyann ítaraṃ jātávedasam / táṃ harāmi pitṛyajñā́ya deváṃ sá gharmám invāt paramé sadhásthe //*
[95] *kurmás ta ā́yur ajáraṃ yád agne yáthā yuktó jātavedo ná ríṣyāḥ / áthā vahāsi sumanasyámāno bhāgáṃ devébhyo havíṣaḥ sujāta //*
[96] *prá deváṃ devyā́ dhiyā́ bháratā jātávedasam / havyā́ no vakṣad ānuṣák //*
[97] *yā́ rúco jātávedaso devatrā́ havyavā́hanīḥ / tā́bhir no yajñám invatu //*
[98] *jātávedase sunavāma sómam arātīyató ní dahāti védaḥ / sá naḥ parṣad áti durgā́ṇi víśvā nāvéva síndhuṃ duritā́ty agníḥ //*
[99] *víśvāni no durgáhā jātavedaḥ síndhuṃ ná nāvā́ duritā́ti parṣi / ágne atriván námasā gṛṇānò 'smā́kam bodhy avitā́ tanū́nām //*
[100] *ā́ nā́mabhir marúto vakṣi víśvān ā́ rūpébhir jātavedo huvānáḥ / yajñáṃ gíro jaritúḥ suṣṭutíṃ ca víśve ganta maruto víśva ūtī́ //*

Jātavedas is said to be some kinds of officiant: Hotṛ, Ṛtvij, and Purohita.

RV 1.127.1 I consider Agni as *the Hotṛ*, the bounteous god, the son of strength, Jātavedas, like an inspired one, Jātavedas, the god who performs sacrifice well with the upward figure directed to the gods. With the glitter, he desires the flaming of Ghṛta and the offered Sarpis[101].

RV 2.2.1 Increase Agni Jātavedas with sacrifice, sacrifice continually with the oblation and the song of praise for the flaming, well regaled one who gives sunshine, *the Hotṛ* of heaven, who is on the pole [of the carriage] at the sacrificial enclosures[102].

RV 6.15.7 With a song of praise I praise Agni, who is kindled by the fire-wood. [I appoint him], who is pure and clear, as *the Purohita*[103] constantly at the sacrifice. With the hymns, we implore Jātavedas, [namely] *the inspired Hotṛ*, the seer, who is rich in gifts and free from malice[104].

RV 8.71.11 [Our songs of praise are to] Agni Jātavedas, the son of might, who is always the immortal among the mortals, *the pleasant Hotṛ* at the settlement, for the giving of wealth[105].

RV 10.88.4 Agni Jātavedas, who was *the first Hotṛ*, who was loved by the gods, and whom the chosen ones anointed with

---

[101] *agníṃ hótāram manye dā́svantaṃ vásuṃ sūnúṃ sáhaso jātávedasaṃ vípraṃ ná jātávedasam / yá ūrdhváyā svadhvaró devó devā́cyā kṛpā́ / ghṛtásya víbhrāṣṭim ánu vaṣṭi śocíṣājúhvānasya sarpíṣaḥ //*

[102] *yajñéna vardhata jātávedasam agníṃ yajadhvaṃ havíṣā tánā girā́ / samidhānáṃ suprayásaṃ svàrṇaraṃ dyukṣáṃ hótāraṃ vṛjáneṣu dhūrṣádam //*

[103] Geldner: "zum Vorsitzer".

[104] *sámiddham agníṃ samídhā girā́ gṛṇe śúcim pāvakám puró adhvaré dhruvám / vípraṃ hótāram puruvā́ram adrúhaṃ kavíṃ sumnaír īmahe jātávedasam //*

[105] *agníṃ sūnúṃ sáhaso jātávedasaṃ dānā́ya vā́ryāṇām / dvitā́ yó bhū́d amṛ́to mártyeṣv ā́ hótā mandrátamo viśí //*

	the Ājya, strengthen whatever flies, walks, stays and goes[106].
RV 5.22.2	Put down Agni Jātavedas, [namely] *the divine Ṛtvij*. Let sacrifice, which comprehends the gods, go [to him] today one after another[107].
RV 5.26.7	Put down Agni Jātavedas, [namely] the conveyor of the oblations, the youngest one, *the divine Ṛtvij*[108].
RV 3.2.8	Worship him, who gives the oblation, and who performs the sacrifice well. Honour domestic Jātavedas. Agni, the active charioteer of the great regular order, became *the Purohita of the gods*[109].
RV 6.10.1	Appoint your agreeable, divine, well-praised Agni as *the Purohita*[110] at sacrifice, when sacrifice is going on. Appoint him with the Ukthas, because he is our illuminator. Jātavedas will carry out good sacrifices[111].

While Jātavedas is often said to be a conveyor and an officiant, there is no statement that Vaiśvānara should bring the oblations to the gods or that he should be an officiant at a sacrifice. Geldner translates RV 6.7.3cd *vaíśvānara tvám asmā́su dhehi vásūni rājan spṛhayā́yyāṇi* "Bring du, Vaiśvānara, uns begehrenswerte Schätze, o king". However, the verb is *dhehi*, which does not imply that Vaiśvānara literally "brings" something. RV 7.5.5 *rayīṇā́ṃ vaiśvānarám* is translated "den Wagenlenker der Reichtümer" by Geldner. However, 6.7.2 *vaiśvānaráṃ rathyàm adhvarā́ṇāṃ*, 10.92.1 *yajñásya vo rathyàṃ (agním)*, 8.44.27 *yajñā́nāṃ rathyè (agnáye)*, 8.45.7 *rathī́tamo rathī́nām (índraḥ)*, etc. show that *rathī́* "chariot-rider" should be interpreted as "leader" or "commander" in this

---

[106] *yó hótā́sīt prathamó devájuṣṭo yáṃ samā́ñjann ā́jyenā vṛṇānā́ḥ / sá patatrī̀tvaráṃ sthā́ jágad yác chvātrám agnír akṛṇoj jātávedāḥ //*

[107] *ny àgníṃ jātávedasaṃ dádhātā devám ṛtvíjam / prá yajñá etv ānuṣág adyā́ devávyacastamaḥ //*

[108] *ny àgníṃ jātávedasaṃ hotravā́haṃ yáviṣṭhyam / dádhātā devám ṛtvíjam //*

[109] *namasyáta havyádātiṃ svadhvaráṃ duvasyáta dámyaṃ jātávedasam / rathī́r ṛtásya bṛható vícarṣaṇir agnír devā́nām abhavat puróhitaḥ //*

[110] Geldner: "Bestellet ... zum Vorsitzer".

[111] *puró vo mandráṃ divyáṃ suvṛktím prayatí yajñé agním adhvaré dadhidhvam / purá ukthébhiḥ sá hí no vibhā́vā svadhvarā́ karati jātávedāḥ //*

context, and not as "carrier"[112]. In any case, *rátha* is not a carriage, but a chariot.

If these functions were those of Agni in general, they would also appear in the Vaiśvānara verses. From this fact we can deduce that the functions as a conveyor and an officiant are particular to Jātavedas (~V ∩ J), and not to Agni in general. Findly (1981: 364) indicated a function of Jātavedas as the conveyor of corpses. This function should be understood as a part of the general function as a conveyor.

In the following verse, Vaiśvānara is said to be a drinking vessel for the gods:

RV 6.7.1 The gods create Vaiśvānara, [namely] the Agni who is born regularly, the head of heaven, the spoke-god of earth, the seer, the universal king, the guest of the people, *the drinking-vessel at the mouth*[113].

"Trough" in the next verse must be describing the same thing.

RV 6.7.2 The gods rejoice together at the navel of the sacrifices, the seat of wealth, *the great trough*. The gods create Vaiśvānara, the chariot-wheel[114] of the sacrifices, the banner of the sacrifice[115].

Vaiśvānara is the sun, and Jātavedas moves between heaven and earth to carry the oblations. And here Vaiśvānara is said to be a drinking vessel or a great trough. It is reasonable to think that the oblations which are thrown into the sacrificial fire are carried through the Antarikṣa by Jātavedas, and given to the gods at Vaiśvānara. Considering that Jātavedas does not have the function of "great trough", this could be accepted as a particular function of Vaiśvānara.

In the following verse, Jātavedas is said to be "brought" by the flames:

RV 1.50.1 The flames bring the god Jātavedas upwards, so that everyone can see Sūrya[116].

---

[112] Mayrhofer *rathī́* "Wagenlenker, Wagenkämpfer" under *rátha*.

[113] *mūrdhā́naṃ divó aratím pṛthivyā́ vaiśvānarám ṛtá ā́ jātám agním / kavíṃ samrā́jam átithiṃ jánānām āsánn ā́ pā́traṃ janayanta devā́ḥ //*

[114] *rathyàṃ adhvarā́ṇāṃ* is not perfectly clear. If we start from Mayrhofer's "Wagenrad", we might be able to imagine the whole Agni structure which rotates like a chariot-wheel.

[115] *nā́bhiṃ yajñā́nāṃ sádanaṃ rayīṇā́m mahā́m āhāvám abhí sáṃ navanta / vaiśvānaráṃ rathyàm adhvarā́ṇāṃ yajñásya ketúṃ janayanta devā́ḥ //*

[116] *úd u tyáṃ jātávedasaṃ deváṃ vahanti ketávaḥ / dṛśé víśvāya sū́ryam //*

This is not contradictory with the result of our research. Here, Jātavedas is pushed up from the fire altar, and it supports the rise of the sun as the spoke-god.

Vaiśvānara-Jātavedas

Rigveda contains 4 verses which mention Vaiśvānara and Jātavedas in one verse:

RV 1.59.5	O Jātavedas Vaiśvānara, your greatness surpasses the great heaven. You are the king of the settlements of mankind. Through the battle, you made room[117] for the gods[118].
RV 6.8.1	Now, I praise the strength and wisdom of Jātavedas, [namely] the strong, reddish bull. For Vaiśvānara the new hymn purifies himself, just like the pure soma which is dear to Agni[119].
RV 7.5.8	O Agni Vaiśvānara Jātavedas, procure us with the excellent tonic with which you cause to swell your present, the great fame for a pious mortal[120].
RV 7.13.2	O Agni, flaming with your flame, being born, you filled heaven and earth. O Vaiśvānara Jātavedas, you liberated the gods from the imprecation with your greatness[121].

Logically spoken, these verses must have the attributes which belong to V $\cup$ J. But here we see no special characteristics of Vaiśvānara or Jātavedas[122]. We will return to some of these verses in Chapter 2.

---

[117] Geldner: "Freiheit". Maryhofer (under *váras*): "freier, hindernisloser Raum, Freiraum".

[118] *diváś cit te bṛható jātavedo vaíśvānara prá ririce mahitvám / rā́jā kṛṣṭīnā́m asi mā́nuṣīṇāṃ yudhā́ devébhyo várivaś cakartha //*

[119] *pṛkṣásya vṛ́ṣṇo aruṣásya nū́ sáhaḥ prá nú vocaṃ vidáthā jātávedasaḥ / vaiśvānarā́ya matír návyasī śúciḥ sóma iva pavate cā́rur agnáye //*

[120] *tā́m agne asmé íṣam érayasva vaíśvānara dyumátīṃ jātavedaḥ / yáyā rā́dhaḥ pínvasi viśvavāra pṛthú śrávo dāśúṣe mártyāya //*

[121] *tvám agne śocíṣā śóśucāna ā́ ródasī apṛṇā jā́yamānaḥ / tvám devā́m̐ abhíśaster amuñco vaíśvānara jātavedo mahitvā́ //*

[122] The attributes which are juxtaposed with Vaiśvānara and Jātavedas in these verses are as follows: *rā́jā kṛṣṭīnā́ṃ mā́nuṣāṃām* (king of the races of

Agni

The attributes of Vaiśvānara and Jātavedas are sometimes mentioned by the name of Agni.

According to the results of our research, the Agni mentioned in the following two verses must be Jātavedas, because he is called Purohita, Ṛtvij, and Hotṛ. He is also said to bring the gods.

---

mankind), *pṛkṣásya vŕṣṇo aruṣásya* (strong, reddish bull), *śocíṣā śóśucānáḥ* (flaming with flame), *jā́yamānaḥ* (being born). The element "king" belongs to both V and J. In the Vaiśvānara verses: *rā́jan* RV 1.98.1 (king of beings), 6.8.4 (praiseworthy king), 1.59.3 (king of those who are in mountains), *samrā́j* 6.7.1 (universal king), *páti* 7.5.5 (lord of the folks), *sátpati* 5.27.1 (righteous lord), *vratapā́* 6.8.2 (protector of the law), *sómagopā* 10.45.12 (protector of soma), *rakṣitṛ́* 6.7.7 (protector of the immortal), *abhiśrī́* 1.98.1 (king of beings). In the Jātavedas verses: *rā́jan* 6.15.13 (king), *śréṣṭha* 1.44.4 (chief), *ī́śāna* 1.79.4 (ruler of the booty of cows), *viśpáti* 3.3.8 (lord of kinsmen) *supráṇīti* 3.15.4 (leader of a great sheep-herd). The element "bull" also belongs to both V and J. In the Vaiśvānara verses: *vŕṣan* 3.2.11 (bull), *vṛṣabhá* 1.59.6 (bull). In the Jātavedas verses: *vŕṣan* 3.1.20 (bull), *vṛṣabhá* 3.15.4 (bull). The element "flaming / shining" also belongs to both V and J. In the Vaiśvānara verses: *svàrvat* 1.59.4 (shining), *svarvíd* 3.3.5 (bestowing light), 3.3.10 (bestowing light), 3.26.1 (bestowing light), *śóśucāna* 7.5.3 (flaming for Purus), *vibhā́van* 1.59.7 (shining), *viśvaśúc* 7.13.1 (all-enlighting), *dīdivás* 10.88.14 (shining), *pṛthupā́jas* 3.22.11 (resplendent), 3.3.1 (resplendent), *candrá* 3.3.5 (shining), *suśrī́* 3.3.5 (splendid), *vicakṣaṇá* 3.3.10 (bright), *hárivrata* 3.3.5 (whose surroundings are yellowish), *jyótis* 1.59.2 (light for Āryas). In the Jātavedas verses: *citrábhānu* 10.51.3 (glittering), *atirócamāna* 10.51.3 (shining), *vibhā́van* 6.4.2 (illuminator), 6.10.1 (illuminator), *śukráśocis* 7.14.1 (brightly shining), *sudyótman* 2.4.1 (shining), *rócamāna* 4.14.1 (shining). The element "being born" also belongs to both Vaiśvānara and Jātavedas. In the Vaiśvānara verses: *jātá* 1.98.1 (being born from here), 3.3.10 (being born), 7.13.3 (being born), 6.7.1 (being born regularly), *jā́yamāna* 6.7.5 (being born in the lap of parents), 6.8.2 (being born), 6.9.1 (being born). In the Jātavedas verses: *jā́yamāna* 7.5.7 (being born in the highest heaven). The other facts which can be extracted from these verses are difficult to discern from accidental, poetic expressions, but they are within the range of V $\cap$ J: "whose greatness surpasses the great heaven", "making room for the gods through the battle", "procuring with exellent tonic", "filling the heaven and the earth", "liberating the gods from the misfortune".

RV 1.1.1	I invoke Agni, the Purohita, the divine Ṛtvij of the sacrifice, the Hotṛ, the best bestower of wealth[123].
RV 1.1.2	Agni, who is to be invoked by past and present seers, will carry the gods here[124].

The Agni mentioned in the following verse must be Vaiśvānara, if "who appears shining at the twilight" denotes the morning sun.

RV 1.1.7	To you, o Agni who appears shining at the twilight, day by day we come with the hymns bringing homage[125].

In the following verse, no particular attribute of Vaiśvānara or Jātavedas is stated.

RV 1.1.9	So, o Agni, be easy of access to us, as a father to his son. Go together with us for well-being[126].

As is clear from the above, the Agni verses are a mixture of the verses for Vaiśvānara and Jātavedas. So we can conclude that the Agni mentioned here is an unspecified, undifferentiated Agni, which includes Agni Vaiśvānara, Agni Jātavedas, and Agni in general. Therefore: 1) When fire is called Vaiśvānara, the attributes of Agni in general and the particular attributes of Vaiśvānara are meant. 2) When fire is called Jātavedas, the attributes of Agni in general and the particular attributes of Jātavedas are meant. 3) When fire is called simply Agni, the attributes of Vaiśvānara, Jātavedas and Agni in general are meant.

Agni, Agni Vaiśvānara, Agni Jātavedas

As a result of our research, we have made the following clear: 1) In terms of the spatial structure, the sun belongs to the core attributes of Vaiśvānara. Jātavedas has no own spatial attributes. 2) In terms of the functions, Jātavedas carries oblations from the fire altar to heaven, and Vaiśvānara functions as a great trough for the gods.

---

[123] *agním ī̱ḷe puróhitaṃ yajñásya devám ṛtvíjam / hótāraṃ ratnadhā́tamam //*
[124] *agníḥ pū́rvebhir ṛ́ṣibhir ī́ḍyo nū́tanair utá / sá devā́m̐ éhá vakṣati //*
[125] *úpa tvāgne divé-dive dóṣāvastar dhiyā́ vayám / námo bháranta émasi //*
[126] *sá naḥ pitéva sūnávé 'gne sūpāyanó bhava / sácasvā naḥ svastáye //*

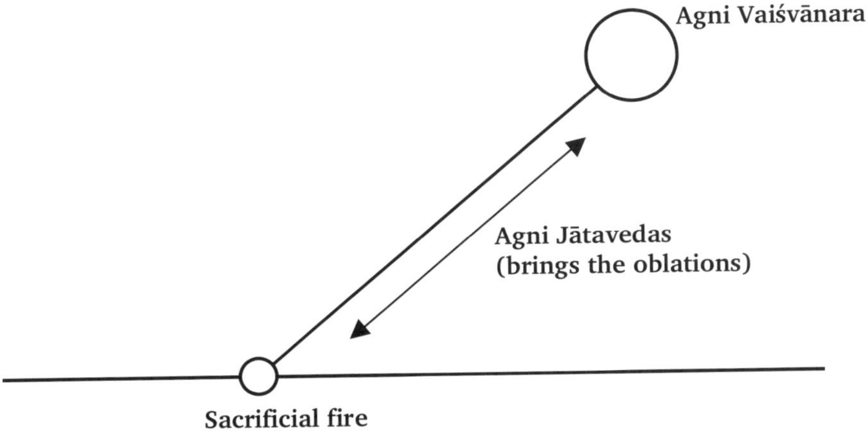

Therefore when we articulate the total structure of Agni through the regional differences, we obtain Vaiśvānara in heaven, Jātavedas between heaven and earth. This perfectly agrees with Bṛhaddevatā.

location	*the form of fire*
Heaven	Agni Vaiśvānara
Antarikṣa	Agni Jātavedas
Earth	Agni

However, the fact that some attributes of Agni in general, e.g. being the spoke-god or the sacrificial fire, are mentioned in the Vaiśvānara verses seems to have some meaning. It means that Vaiśvānara is a part of the cosmic Agni, which forms a continuum spread from heaven to earth. In this structure, the spoke and the sacrificial fire must have been thought of as marginal parts of Vaiśvānara by Vedic Indians. In this point, the Vaiśvānara verses make an interesting contrast with Jātavedas verses. While the cosmic aspect of Agni is conspicuous in the former, the stress is strongly laid on the ritual in the latter. Jātavedas is often invoked as a priest or an oblation-carrier, and he is never identified with the sun. In the above research, we only saw the forms and functions of Vaiśvānara and Jātavedas, and not their "character". But if we are allowed to characterize these manifestations of Agni, we should do it with the words "cosmic" and "ritualistic".

By the late Brāhmaṇa period, the knowledge about Vaiśvānara's spatial location had been lost. It is clear even from a single example from ŚB: 1.4.1.10 "Videgha Māthava held Agni Vaiśvānara in his mouth[127]." This well known story of Videgha Māthava is explained by Heesterman

---

[127] *videghó ha māthávo 'gníṃ vaiśvānaráṃ múkhe babhāra.*

(1993: 30) as the domestication of the wild[128], and it coincides with Findly (1982), who indicated an aspect of the Rigvedic Vaiśvānara "conquering fire". Heesterman further indicates that Agni Vaiśvānara represents the hierarchic aspect of the ruler against the people[129]. It is plausible that Vaiśvānara in the Brāhmaṇa period attained a stronger relationship with the kingship. In any case, the Rigvedic Vaiśvānara and the post-Rigvedic Vaiśvānara must be considered separately. The post-Rigvedic Vaiśvānara does not have some attributes of the Rigvedic Vaiśvānara, and it also acquired some other attributes. A separate study is necessary for the post-Rigvedic Vaiśvānara.

In Section 2 of this paper, we will observe whether the knowledge about the spatial location of Vaiśvānara is preserved in the verbal procedure of the cremation ritual.

The Names *vaiśvānará* and *jātávedas*

It might now be worthwhile discussing the meaning of the names *vaiśvānará* and *jātávedas*.

Traditionally, *vaiśvānará* has been interpreted as "belonging to all men"[130]. Instead of this interpretation, Kuiper (1951) derives *-nara* from the old root **ner* "vital strength" and interprets the compound as "related to him, who possesses the total amount of vital strength". Gonda (1959: 95) is somewhat sceptic about it, and Findly (1982: 5) rejects it because "there is little if any use of **ner* "vital strength" ... out of compound in the Rigveda". I do not adopt Kuiper's interpretation for the same reason as Gonda and Findly. De Vries (1979) proposes the third possibility "associated with all fires" based on statements of ŚB, but it does not seem to be very meaningful. In ŚB, Vaiśvānara is identified with almost everything to explain sacrificial procedures, so it cannot be the basis of a discussion.

---

[128] Heesterman summarizes the story and argues: "But the real way to conquer the other world of the wild is, of course, through the fire, as is shown by the story of Māthava Videgha and the fire, Agni Vaiśvānara ("common to all men"), that he held inside himself. His brahmin priest, however, teased it out of his mouth by mentioning ghee in a fire-kindling mantra. On the stimulus of the word "ghee" the fire flashed forth and rolled on to the east, burning everything before it, until it came to a stop at the Sadānīrā River ... "At that time that [land] was quite uncultivated and waterlogged, for it had not [yet] been tasted by Agni Vaiśvānara. Nowadays, however, it is fully cultivated, for the brahmins have caused [Agni] to taste it through sacrifices." So the sacrificial fire is the primary tool for domesticating the wild." See also p.124, where the same story is cited.

[129] Heesterman (1993) p. 89.

[130] Macdonell (1897: 99), Oldenberg (1917: 62, 123), Keith (1925: 164).

I support the traditional "belonging to all men". However, I would like to suggest a special implication which is contained in this concept. "Belonging to all men" can be interpreted in two ways: "common, in the sense that it is not personally owned by anyone" and "common, in the sense that everyone has it in himself".

The Rigvedic Agni Vaiśvānara is not personally owned by anyone: While every sacrificial fire personally belongs to a sacrificer, the sun does not belong to anyone. It is an impersonal fire, which is shared by all the sacrificers[131]. Thus the sun is called *vaiśvānara*. Note that this name is derived from the contrast with the personal sacrificial fire, not from the contrast with the other kinds of fire, e.g. wild fire or cooking fire[132].

As mentioned above, in ŚB we see Agni Vaiśvānara personally held by Videgha Māthava, which seems to imply that Agni Vaiśvānara was losing its impersonal character. In BĀU 5.9, it is even identified with the digesting fire. Here, *vaiśvānara* obviously means "common in the sense that everyone has it in himself", which shows that the meaning of the word *vaiśvānara* changed in the post-Rigvedic period[133].

The name *jātávedas* has long been a mystery. The first part of this compound has two possibilities. As an adjective, it might mean "born". And as a noun it might mean "creature". The last part also has two meanings. As a derivative from *vid* (find / have), it might mean "possession".

---

[131] We might be able to understand the following verse as a visual image of the sacrificial fires focussing on Vaiśvānara: RV 1.59.1 *vayā́ íd agne agnáyas te anyé tvé víśve amŕ̥tā mādayante / vaíśvānara nā́bhir asi kṣitīnā́ṃ sthū́ṇeva jánām̐ upamíd yayantha //* "O Agni, other fires are only your branches. All the immortals rejoice at you. O Vaiśvānara, you are the navel of the settlements. You hold the people like a supporting pillar."

[132] The development of the speculation about *ātmán* could be understood clearly by means of the contrast between the sacrificial fire and Agni Vaiśvānara:

The personal fires	:	The common fire
The personal souls	:	x

The solution must be: x = the common soul (Ātman Vaiśvānara). At this point, our discussion comes close to that of Heesterman (1964 and 1993). See especially Heesterman (1993: 215ff), where he discusses the interiorization of fire.

[133] Curiously, the term Ātman Vaiśvānara (ChU 5.11.1-5.18.2) seems to preserve the original meaning of *vaiśvānará*. (Note that nothing personal is identified with Ātman Vaiśvānara in the discussion between Uddālaka Āruṇi and the scholars.) This might mean that this term has an old origin, though it had not been documented. See also the discussion about Vaiśvānara in ŚB 10.6.1.

As a derivative from *vid* (know), it might mean "knowledge". Based on the combinations of these, most scholars interpret it as "all-knower" or "all-possessor"[134]. Apart from these interpretations, Macdonell (1897: 97) cites the following verse, and argues that *jātávedas* means "he who knows all the generations":

RV 6.15.13 Agni is the Hotṛ, the householder. He is the king. *Jātavedas knows all the births*. Let the regular one, who sacrifices the best among the gods and the mortals, sacrifice[135].

Findly (1981) admits two possibilities "*adj*. born, innate" and "*n*. creature" for *jātá*, and only one possibility "possession" for *védas*. She further determines the meaning of the compound *jātávedas* through examining the context of the Jātavedas verses, and observes: "The full range of Jātavedas themes centers on his immediacy in the worshipper's home as the focus of an on-going ritual life, and the resulting sense that Jātavedas, being present over time, is both witness and guardian to the passing of the generations. It is quite natural, then, that the range of his concern should extend into the Pitaras, for the continuity of the lineage into the future through offspring ... is guaranteed only by the soundness of the lineage in the past is based, in turn, upon the ever-present protection of the dying worshipper, through death and the flames of the cremation fire, to the abode of the pious beyond[136]". After this discussion, she concludes that *jātá* in the compound means "what has been born".

As the title of Findly's paper "Jātavedas in the Ṛgveda: The God of Generations" shows, she largely follows Macdonell's line and has supplied it with an etymological basis and a detailed contextual study. Most of her discussion is acceptable, but as to the interpretation of *jātá*, there is another possibility: The word *jātá* can also mean "birth". When we use this meaning, then we get "the possessor/knower of the birth" as the meaning of *jātávedas*. This gives a more direct and clear basis to Macdonell's "he who knows all the generations".

As Findly (1981: 359) discusses, Jātavedas is associated with wealth. Within our scheme, this can be explained as the result of his being a conveyor. The following verse is a typical example, in which he brings gifts from gods to "the pious one":

---

[134] As to the various proposals in secondary literature, see Findly (1981: 349ff). Mayrhofer: "der Kenntnis (*vedas-*) von den Wesen (*jātá-*, o. I 567) hat".

[135] *agnír hótā gṛhápatiḥ sá rā́jā víśvā veda jánimā jātávedāḥ / devā́nām utá yó mártyānāṃ yájiṣṭhaḥ sá prá yajatām ṛtā́vā //*

[136] Findly (1981) pp.371-372

RV 6.5.3 You sit from of old in these clans. With magical power, you were the charioteer of wealth. Therefore, o wise Jātavedas, *you send forth wealth one after another for the pious one*[137].

The "wealth" here primarily means cattle[138]. He is concerned with the birth of cattle, or more precisely, he brings something which is essential for the propagation of cattle.

Jātavedas is said to be a knower[139]. Although there are not many verses which show what he knows, we might be able to infer it from the following verses.

RV 4.3.8 Being asked, how do you answer to the troop of Marut, to the regular order[140], to the great sun, to Aditi, to the powerful one? O Jātavedas, be successful, you, *who knows heaven*[141].

RV 4.5.12 What wealth of him is for us? Is the treasure [for us]? You speak for us, o Jātavedas, *who knows secretly the far [end] of this way for us*[142], [whether] we, being censured, have not taken a deserted[143] way[144].

RV 10.69.9 O Jātavedas, [the fire] of Vadhryaśva, even the immortal gods praise your greatness. When the clans of peo-

[137] *tvám̥ vikṣú pradívaḥ sīda āsú krátvā rathī́r abhavo vā́ryāṇām / áta inoṣi vidhaté cikitvo vy ā̀nuṣág jātavedo vásūni //*

[138] RV 1.79.4 (Jātavedas verse): *vā́jasya gómata ī́śānaḥ* "possessing booty rich in cattle".

[139] The word *cikitvás* (knowing) occurs only with Jātavedas and never with Vaiśvānara. Cf.RV 1.77.5; 3.17.2; 4.3.8; 4.5.12; 6.5.3; 10.110.1.

[140] Otherwise, *marútām ṛtā́ya* could be a result of haplology for *marútām amṛtā́ya.*

[141] *kathā́ śárdhāya marútām ṛtā́ya kathā́ sūré bṛhaté pṛchyámānaḥ / práti bravó 'ditaye turā́ya sā́dhā divó jātavedaś cikitvā́n //*

[142] Geldner: "da das ferne (Ende) dieses unseres Weges im Verborgenen ist". I take *gúhā* as an adverb.

[143] Mayrhofer: "zurückgelassene Fußspur". However, root *REC* "verlassen".

[144] *kím̥ no asyá dráviṇam̥ kád dha rátnam̥ ví no voco jātavedaś cikitvā́n / gúhā́dhvanaḥ paramám̥ yán no asyá réku padám̥ ná nidānā́ áganma //*

ple came inquiring, you won with the people who were strengthened by you[145].

The first verse mentions the knowledge of heaven, the second the secret knowledge of a good pasture, and the third one must be seen from the point of the Brahmodya. These are all connected to the secret knowledge. It seems possible that *jātávedas* originally meant "the possessor of (the secret of) the birth (of cattle)". The meaning was expanded to "the possessor of secret" during the early Rigvedic period. The last expansion happened in the late Rigvedic period with the introduction of cremation. Jātavedas is now regarded as the carrier of the deceased sacrificer.

This interpretation might also shed some light on the following verse:

RV 10.15.13 *You know the fathers who are here or not here, whom we know or do not know, as much as they are.* O Jātavedas, enjoy the well-made sacrifice with the refreshment[146].

He knows every *pitṛ*, namely his rebirth in heaven. What he knows is not fragmental information such as tomorrow's weather, but the whole system of birth and rebirth.

To Heaven

The cremation (BPS 1.8) is carried out with some mantra-recitations and offerings. Our initial problem was the functions of the three forms of Agni that are invoked in these mantras. In the first section of this paper, we have made clear the total spatial / functional structure of Agni. In this section we are going to substantiate the process of ascension with the schema.

The main procedures described in the text of BPS 1.8 are as follows[147]:

1. The ignition of the corpse with Mantra 1.
2. Mantra 2.
3. Mantra 3 (Ṣaḍḍhotṛ-mantra).
4. Tying a goat with Mantra 4.
5. An offering with Mantra 5.

---

[145] *devā́ś cit te amŕ̥tā jātavedo mahimā́naṃ vādhryaśva prá vocan / yát sampŕ̥cham mā́nuṣīr víśa ā́yan tvā́ṃ nŕ̥bhir ajayas tvā́vṛdhebhiḥ //*

[146] *yé cehá pitáro yé ca néhá yā́ṃś ca vidmá yā́m̐ u ca ná pravidmá / tvā́ṃ vettha yáti té jātavedaḥ svadhā́bhir yajñā́ṃ súkṛtaṃ juṣasva //*

[147] For the description of the ritual, see Caland (1896). This procedure is described in p. 58ff. For the translation, see Śrautakośa Volume I English Section Part II, p.1049.

6. The oblation of avadānas.
7. The worship of the deceased.

Mantras 1-5 are taken from TĀ 6.1.4[148]:

Mantra 1	O Agni, let you not burn him completely. Let you not consume him. Let you not destroy the skin, nor the body. When you have made him cooked, o Jātavedas, then send him to the fathers[149].
Mantra 2	When you have made him cooked, o Jātavedas, then give him over to the fathers. When he would go to this leader of life[150], then he will be subject to the gods[151].
Mantra 3	Let your eye go to the sun. The body[152] to the wind. Go to heaven and earth at will. Or go to the water. If your welfare is there, abide in the plants with the bones[153].
Mantra 4	The goat is [your] share[154]. Heat it with the heat. Let your heat heat it. Let your flame [heat] it. O Jātavedas,

[148] Mantras 1-4 are RV 10.16.1, 10.16.2, 10.16.3, 10.16.4.

[149] *maínam agne ví daho mā́bhí śoco mā́sya tvácaṃ cikṣipo mā́ śárīram / yadā́ śṛtáṃ kṛṇávo jātavedó 'them enam prá hiṇutāt pitṛ́bhyaḥ //*

[150] *Asunīti*: As to the suffix *-ti* in agent nouns, cf. AiG II,2 p636. Schlerath (1968) gives the translation "asu-Führung"(p148-149), but Bodewitz (1991) suggests correctly: "The *asunīti* of the Ṛgvedasaṃhitā refers to the same situation as described in the story of Sāvitrī, where Yama or his messengers are said to fetch (*netum*) the soul. The dictionaries misinterpret this compound and often make it refer to the realm of the dead." I would interpret the *ásunīti* of this context as Agni Jātavedas.

[151] *śṛtáṃ yadā́ kárasi jātavedó 'them enam pári dattāt pitṛ́bhyaḥ / yadā́ gáchāty ásunītim etā́m áthā devā́nāṃ vaśanī́r bhavāti //*

[152] I translate *ātmán* and *śárīra* here "body" and "bones" respectively. The other version of the Ṣaḍḍhotṛ-mantra (TĀ 3.4.1) is: "Your eye [goes to] the sun. The prāṇa, [to] the wind. The back, [to] the heaven. The body (*ātma*) [to] the Antarikṣa. With the limbs, [to] the sacrifice. With the bones (*śarīraiḥ*), [to] the earth."

[153] *sū́ryaṃ cákṣur gachatu vā́tam ātmā́ dyā́ṃ ca gacha pṛthivī́ṃ ca dhármaṇā / apó vā gacha yádi tátra te hitám óṣadhīṣu práti tiṣṭhā śárīraiḥ //*

[154] TĀ: *ajó 'bhāgás*, while Caland's text of BPS and RV are without avagraha. RV: *ajó bhāgás*. The accent of TĀ text seems to be impossible. This might be a simple mistake by the editor.

bring him to the world of the pious with your auspicious body[155].

Mantra 5[156] You are this man. Here, you are from him. Yonder, you are the womb for him. Vaiśvānara is the son who creates the world for the father. O Jātavedas, bring him to the world of well-doers[157].

The meaning of these mantras is relatively clear. There is almost no need for commentary except Mantra 3. Many scholars interpret that the deceased sacrificer is said to go to heaven, earth, water, and plants[158]. However, Macdonell (1897: 166) noticed a problem: "In one passage of the RV. (10.16.3) the eye of the dead man is called upon to go to the sun and his breath (*ātmā*) to the wind. But this notion, occuring in the midst of verses which refer to Agni as conducting the deceased to the other world, can only be an incidental fancy, suggested perhaps by the speculations about Puruṣa (10.90.13), where the eye of the latter becomes the sun and his breath the wind. In the same passage (also in 10.58.7) the soul is spoken of as going to the waters or the plants, a conception which perhaps contains the germ of the theory of metempsychosis." Concerning this problem, I would like to suggest that this peculiarity of Mantra 3 is caused by the interpretation of the second person: 1) Throughout this series of mantras, the second person and two kinds of third person *ena-* and *ta-* are consistently used to denote Agni, the deceased, and the goat, respectively. Although it is not impossible to think that only Mantra 3 denotes a different person with "you", it seems much more natural to take it as Agni. 2) The following verse from TB corresponds to Mantra 3:

TB 1.2.1.21 – 22 For energy and power, I lift you up. For virile vigour, for long life, for brilliance. You are a beater of rival, beater of Vṛtra. Your heavenly greatness which is among gods, your body, which entered into cattles, your prosperity, which spread among humans — therewith, o Agni, rejoicing, come to us. From heaven, from earth, from the Antarikṣa, from wind, from cattles,

---

[155] *ajó bhāgás tápasā tám̐ tapasva tám̐ te śocís tapatu tám̐ te arcíḥ / yā́s te śivā́s tanvò jātavedas tā́bhir vahainam̐ sukŕ̥tām ulokám //*

[156] Cf. Bodewitz (1973) p128-130.

[157] *ayám̐ vái tvám asmā́d ádhi tvám etád ayám̐ vái tád asya yónir asi / vaiśvānaráḥ putráḥ pitré lokakŕ̥j jātavedo vahemám̐ sukŕ̥tām̐ yátra lokā́ḥ //*

[158] E.g. Oldenberg (1894) p.530 note 1, Hillebrandt (1902) p.417, Horsch (1971) p.112ff.

from plants. From whatever place where you were born, o Agni, rejoicing, come to us.[159].

This verse is recited at the establishment of the fire in the Agnyādheya ritual[160]. Here, Agni is called from heaven, earth, Antarikṣa, wind, animals, and plants towards the fire altar. It is highly possible that the recitation of this TB mantra is intended as the reconstruction of the fire which has been dispersed in the cremation[161]. In this case, "you" in our Mantra 3 must be Agni. 3) All the places mentioned in Mantra 3 (sun, wind, heaven, earth, waters, plants) are well known as Agni's places.

On the other hand, the traditional interpretation of Mantra 3 is supported by RV 10.58, in which "your mind" (*te ... mánas*) is called back from various places, especially from Yama's place (1), heaven or earth (2), waters or plants (7), sun or dawn (8). BĀU 3.2.13 (a question from Ārtabhāga to Yājñavalkya) also tells that the voice, breath, eye, mind, hearing, body, soul, hairs of the head, hairs of the body, blood and semen of the deceased person go to fire, wind, sun, moon, quarters of heaven, earth, space, plants, trees, and waters, respectively. However, the deceased is brought forth by Agni's manifestation. It means that he goes wherever Agni goes. Therefore the concept of RV 10.58 can be explained as a derivative from RV 10.16.3 (our Mantra 3). While TB 1.2.1.21-22, which is concerned with the reconstruction of the dispersed fire, preserves the original concept of RV 10.16.3, BĀU 3.2.13 adopted the concept of RV 10.58, in which the focus is shifted to the deceased person.

As already seen, the usual oblations are put into the sacrificial fire, are brought to heaven by Jātavedas, and then they are enjoyed by the gods at Vaiśvānara. In these cremation mantras, this system of Agni functions in exactly the same way as in normal oblations. In Mantra 1, Agni and Agni Jātavedas are invoked. According to our schema, this is the sacrificial fire and the Jātavedas, respectively. The body of the deceased is ignited during this mantra, and then it is brought to heaven by Jātavedas as a conveyor during Mantras 2, 3, and 4.

---

[159] *ójase bálāya tvódyacche / vŕ̥ṣaṇe śúṣmāyā́yuṣe várcase / sapatnatū́r asi vṛtratū́ḥ / yás te devéṣu mahimā́ suvargáḥ // yás ta ātmā́ paśúṣu práviṣṭaḥ / púṣṭir yā́ te mánuṣyeṣu prathé / táyā no agne juṣámāṇa éhi / diváḥ pṛthivyā́ḥ páry antárikṣāt / vātāt paśúbhyo ádhi óṣadhībhyaḥ / yátra yatra jātavedaḥ sambabhū́va / táto no agne juṣámāṇa éhi /*

[160] Krick (1982) p. 322.

[161] It seems me natural to assume continuity in the rituals of two generations: the cremation of father — the Agnyādheya of the son. Anyway, what we can observe in this correspondence of Agnyādheya and cremation verses is the trace of the ritualistic speculation about the continuity of the fire.

In Mantra 5, the relation between the fire and the sacrificer is explained. In this world (here), the sacrificer makes the sacrificial fire, while in the yonder world the fire (Vaiśvānara) gives him birth. The implication is: Vaiśvānara, the fire in heaven, is the exit on the way from earth to heaven, while the sacrificial fire on earth is the entrance to that way.

The complete picture is now clear. The deceased is burned by the sacrificial fire, and is brought towards heaven by Jātavedas, the conveyor, and finally reaches heaven through Vaiśvānara, the sun. Thus he is not brought by Agni in general, but by Jātavedas. And the way he takes is a particular one which combines heaven and earth, namely the total structure of Agni. The invocations of Agni, Jātavedas and Vaiśvānara in the cremation mantras are therefore not accidental occurrences of arbitrary epithets, but have their own functions in the ritual's procedure.

In this chapter, we treated the mythological structure which forms the background of the Vedic funeral ritual. The above discussion corresponds to the point indicated by the arrow in the concept scheme below.

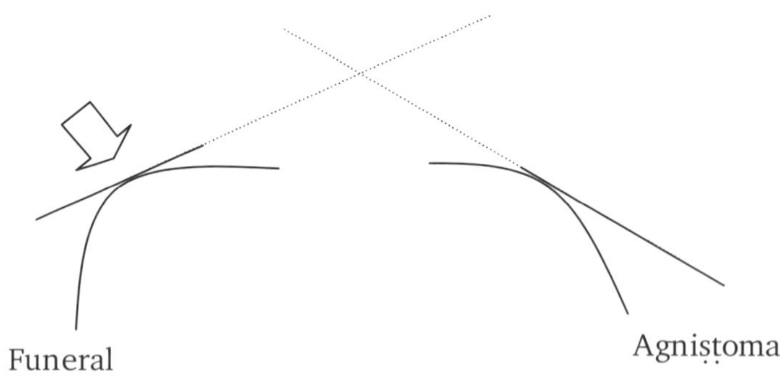

Chapter 2: Descent of Fire

RV 3.3 contains a curious problem concerning Agni.

RV 3.3.11 Because of the marvellous powers of Vaiśvānara, the unique seer[162] released *bṛhat* with the creative power. Agni, who magnifies the parents, [namely] the rich-in-sperm Heaven and Earth, was born[163].

Something which is called *bṛhat* (great/high) is released here. However, what is denoted by this term, and by whom it is released, is not clear.

Oldenberg Noten says: "Der 'Weise' wohl eben Vaiśvānara" and "Zu *bṛhát* wird Subst. zu ergänzen sein... hier wohl etwa *bhā́ḥ*." However, light is always released by Agni Vaiśvānara. The *bṛhat* which is released by "the unique seer" with "the creative power" must be something special.

Geldner suggests two possibilities: "sperm" and "song of praise"[164]. Although his second interpretation is followed by Renou EVP: "le (sacrifiant, ce) poète unique a fait couler le haut (éclat, s'exerçant)", his first interpretation sounds more interesting. If he is right, we could explain Agni's recursive generation from a different perspective. It would also shed some light on the meaning of the curious association between Agni and sperm, which appears sporadically in Saṃhitās and Brāhmaṇas[165]. However, Geldner's note to this verse is not based on a detailed study of related Vedic passages. So it seems me to be a good idea to re-examine Geldner's observaton through the discussion of RV 3.3 and related passages.

I will start with the text and translation of this hymn:

---

[162] Geldner: "einzige Seher". The word *éka* seems to mean *par exellence* here. Cf. RV 7.95.2 *ékācetat sárasvatī nadī́nām*.

[163] *vaiśvānarásya daṃsánābhyo bṛhád áriṇād ékaḥ svapasyáyā kavíḥ / ubhā́ pitárā mahá̄yann ajāyatāgnír dyā́vāpṛthivī́ bhū́riretasā //*

[164] "Zu *bṛhat* ist vielleicht *rétaḥ* zu ergänzen, das zu *áriṇāt* passen würde. Es scheinen sich zwei Möglichkeiten zu ergeben. Entweder das Paradoxon, daß Agni zugleich Vater und Sohn ist (1,69,2). In 1,96,4 heißt er der Erzeuger von Himmel und Erde, 3,25,1 aber deren Sohn. *ab* wäre dann eine leichte Anakoluthie. 'Aus den außerordentlichen Kräften des Vaiśvānara entließ Agni den hohen' (Samen) wäre s.v.a. Agni V. entließ aus seinen außerordentlichen K. den Samen. Ähnliche Redefigur 10,3,2cd; 3,4,1b; 5,3,10c; 7,39,1a. Das zu supplierende *rétaḥ* wird durch das folgende *bhū́riretasā* nahegelegt. Oder der Sänger ist Subjekt. Dann ist gemeint: der einzige Seher ergoß für die *d.* des V. einen hohen (Erguß = Lied)."

[165] Cf. Eliade (1976) p.93ff.

RV 3.3.1 They offer the gift of inspired hymn to Vaiśvānara, who has a wide surface[166], so that [he] should go [down] to the firm grounds[167], for the immortal Agni favours the gods, and he never defiles the orders[168].

RV 3.3.2 As a wonderful messenger, he goes between Heaven and Earth. Being seated, he is the Hotṛ, the Purohita of a man. Being rich in hymns, Agni, who was sent by the gods, makes the high residence prosper[169] day by day[170].

RV 3.3.3 The inspired ones magnify Agni, the banner of sacrifices, the performer of distribution, with insights. The sacrificer desires favours from him, on whom they have united the works [and] songs together[171].

RV 3.3.4 As the father of sacrifices, the Asura of the inspired ones, Vimāna and Vayuna[172] of singers, Agni has entered into Heaven and Earth, which have abundant

---

[166] *pṛthupā́jas*: Geldner: "von breiter Gestalt", Renou EVP: "à la vaste forme-massive". As to *pā́jas*, Thieme (1979): "[sichtbare, Vorder-]Seite".

[167] *dharúṇeṣu gā́tave*: Geldner: "um auf sicherem Grunde zu wandeln". But *dharúṇeṣu* must be the "Localis des Zieles". Renou translates this point correctly: "pour (obtenir d') accéder aux fondements (de l'Ordre sacré)". Cf. also Renou (1958) pp.1-3. However, I see no reason to add "de l'Ordre sacré". Cf. RV 1.52.2 *sá párvato ná dharúṇeṣv ácyutaḥ sahásramūtis táviṣīṣu vāvṛdhe,* "He (Indra), who gives thousands of help, has grown in powers like a mountain immovable on the *dharúṇas*".

[168] *vaiśvānarā́ya pṛthupā́jase vípo rátnā vidhanta dharúṇeṣu gā́tave / agnír hí devā́m̐ amṛ́to duvasyáty áthā dhármāṇi sanátā ná dūduṣat //*

[169] *kṣáyam bṛhántam pári bhūṣati*: Geldner: "nimmt Agni seinen hohen Wohnsitz ein". Renou: "il entoure-de-soins la haute résidence". But Gonda (1959a: 93): "to exert strengthening or favourable influence".

[170] *antár dūtó ródasī dasmá īyate hótā níṣatto mánuṣaḥ puróhitaḥ / kṣáyam bṛhántam pári bhūṣati dyúbhir devébhir agnír iṣitó dhiyā́vasuḥ //*

[171] *ketúṃ yajñā́nāṃ vidáthasya sā́dhanaṃ víprāso agním mahayanta cíttibhiḥ / ápāṃsi yásminn ádhi saṃdadhúr gíras tásmin sumnā́ni yájamāna ā́ cake //*

[172] *vimā́nam* and *vayúnam*: The correct meaning of these words is unknown. Geldner translates *vayúnam* "die Richte", Renou "le repère". Thieme (1949: 23-24) translates it "die Umhegung (der umhegende Schutz)", and proposes "Haus" for *vimā́nam*.

forms. As a seer, who is dear to many, he is pleased with [his] abodes[173] [174].

RV 3.3.5 The gods have put here Agni Vaiśvānara, who is shining, having a shining chariot, being always yellowish[175], who is in the water, the bestower of light, who plunges, who is swift, who is covered by the strength, who is wild, who is splendid[176].

RV 3.3.6 Agni, who performs the multiform sacrifice by means of a hymn, with the gods and Manu's offspring who carry out sacrifices, goes riding in a chariot between [Heaven and Earth] as a quick householder who keeps off imprecations[177].

RV 3.3.7 O Agni, be wakeful during the life which has good offspring. Overflow with strength. Bestow tonic by shining for us[178]. Incite energies and great [vigours][179]. O

---

173 *dhā́mabhiḥ*: Geldner: "um seiner Eigenschaften". Renou: "pour ses formes-institutionnelles". But Gonda (1967: 24): "on account of [its] abodes".

174 *pitā́ yajñā́nām ásuro vipaścítāṃ vimā́nam agnír vayúnaṃ ca vāghátām / ā́ viveśa ródasī bhū́rivarpasā purupriyó bhandate dhā́mabhiḥ kavíḥ //*

175 *hárivratam*: Cf. H.-P. Schmidt (1958) "dessen (Berufs-) Gelübde (es ist,) gelb (zu glänzen)".

176 *candrám agníṃ candrárathaṃ hárivrataṃ vaiśvānarám apsuṣádaṃ svarvídam / vigāháṃ tū́rṇiṃ táviṣībhir ā́vṛtam bhū́rṇiṃ devā́sa ihá suśríyaṃ dadhuḥ //*

177 *agnír devébhir mánuṣaś ca jantúbhis tanvānó yajñám purupéśasaṃ dhiyā́ / rathī́r antár īyate sā́dhadiṣṭibhir jīró dámūnā abhiśasticā́tanaḥ //*

178 *sám iṣo didīhi naḥ*: Geldner: "bring uns Labsal mit deinem Lichte", Renou EVP: "brille (en) nous (conférant) toutes jouissances-rituelles". Cf. RV 3.54.22 *svádasva havyā́ sám íṣo didīhi*, 5.4.2 *sugārhapatyā́ḥ sám íṣo didīhi*.

179 *váyāṃsi jinva bṛhatáś ca*: Oldenberg's note: "Zu *bṛhatáḥ* zu ergänzen *vā́jān*? Aehnlich II,2,7. *vā́jān* Obj. zu *jínva* III,15,6. Uebrigens kann *bṛhatáḥ* trotz des Genus zu *váyāṃsi* gehören; *váyas* empfängt gern Beiwort *bṛhát*. Schwerlich *bṛhatáḥ* Gen. sg. (Caland-Henry 374)". Renou: "Anime les forces-vitales et les hauts (pouvoirs)". Geldner: "Errege Kräfte und zwar große". Klein (1985 Vol 1 Part 1: 127) follows Oldenberg and says: "Geldner's rendition would make this passage completely anomalous among *ca*-syntagms".

watchful one, you are the Uśij[180] of the gods, having good magical powers of the inspired verses[181].

RV 3.3.8 People always praise Jātavedas, the lord of settlements, the young guest, the disposer of hymns, the Uśij for the singers, the banner of sacrifices, energetically with salutation so that [he][182] increases[183].

RV 3.3.9 The shining joyous god Agni with the beautiful chariot has encompassed[184] the residences with strength. We should confirm the observance [185] of the much-nourishing one at home with excellent praises[186].

RV 3.3.10 O Vaiśvānara, I desire your abodes, with which you became the bestower of light, o bright one. Being born, you filled up the worlds, Heaven and Earth. O Agni, you encompass[187] all [the worlds] in yourself[188].

RV 3.3.11 Because of the marvellous powers of Vaiśvānara, the unique seer[189] released *bṛhat* with the creative power.

---

[180] *uśij*: Geldner: "Fürbitter", Renou: "prêtre-modèle".

[181] *ágne járasva svapatyá ā́yuny ūrjā́ pinvasva sám ìṣo didīhi naḥ / váyāṃsi jinva bṛhatáś ca jāgṛva uśíg devā́nām ási sukrátur vipā́m //*

[182] Renou and Geldner take "sacrifice" as the agent of the dative infinitive *vṛdhé*. This might be possible, but if we supplement the agent with a word which appears in this verse, it should be *jātávedas* or *nárah*.

[183] *viśpátiṃ yahvám átithiṃ nárah sádā yantā́raṃ dhīnā́m uśíjaṃ ca vāghátām / adhvarā́ṇāṃ cétanaṃ jātávedasam prá śaṃsanti námasā jūtíbhir vṛdhé //*

[184] *pári babhūva*: Gonda (1959a: 83): "to encompass, surround and to have a propitious influence".

[185] *úpa bhūṣema*: Geldner: "Wir wollen seiner Dienste, des Viellabenden im Hause mit Lobesliedern warten", Renou: "Puissions-nous, nous (autres), veiller-avec-soin sur ses décrets". But Gonda (1959a: 84): "to confirm the ordinances (of the god) with excellent song of praise".

[186] *vibhā́vā deváḥ suráṇaḥ pári kṣitī́r agnír babhūva śávasā sumádrathaḥ / tásya vratā́ni bhūripoṣíṇo vayám úpa bhūṣema dáma ā́ suvṛktíbhiḥ //*

[187] *paribhū́r asi*: Cf. Verse 9 *pári babhūva*.

[188] *vaíśvānara táva dhā́māny ā́ cake yébhiḥ svarvíd ábhavo vicakṣaṇa / jātá ā́pṛṇo bhúvanāni ródasī ágne tā́ víśvā paribhū́r asi tmánā //*

[189] Geldner: "einzige Seher". The word *éka* seems to mean *par exellence* here. Cf. RV 7.95.2 *ékācetat sárasvatī nadī́nāṃ*.

> Agni, who magnifies the parents, [namely] the rich-in-sperm Heaven and Earth, was born.

At first sight, this hymn looks like a collection of verses which has no logical thread. But when we read it carefully, it can be seen that the uses of the present and perfect tenses make a sharp contrast as to the aspects of Agni.

Verses 2, 6, 7 and 8 are related in the present tense. These verses mention Agni's attributes as "Hotṛ", "Purohita", "messenger" (2), "going between [Heaven and Earth]" (6). These are the attributes of the ritual fire Agni Jātavedas[190], which is also invoked in Verse 8. Uśij in Verses 7 and 8 also seems to be a priest. This fact seems to indicate that a ritual is being carried out at the present moment of the poet.

On the other hand, the perfect tense appears in 4abc, 5, 9ab and 10d[191], and these verses mention the cosmic aspects of Agni: "entering into heaven and earth" (4c) and "encompassing the earth" (9 and 10). The Agni mentioned here can be understood as the cosmic fire Agni Vaiśvānara[192], which is mentioned in Verse 5. Note that Verse 5 and the previous 4abc (in the perfect) obviously refer to the cosmogonical situation: the establishment of the cosmic Agni structure[193].

Taking the above facts in consideration, RV 3.3 can be overviewed as follows:

Verse	Actual ritual	Cosmogonical situation
1	Introduction to this hymn.	
2	Agni goes between heaven and earth.	
3ab	Inspired ones magnify Agni.	
3cd	The sacrificer desires favours (of Agni). (*ā cake* has the perfect form, but usually interpreted in the present sense.)	
4abc		Agni entered into heaven

[190] See Chapter 1, section "Functions of Vaiśvānara and Jātavedas".
[191] Except *ā́ cake* in 3cd and 10ab.
[192] See Chapter 1, section "Agni, Agni Vaiśvānara, Agni Jātavedas".
[193] See Chapter 1, especially the figure in the section "Agni, Agni Vaiśvānara, Agni Jātavedas".

		and earth.
4d	Still now, he is pleased with the abodes.	
5		The cosmic fire was established.
6-8	Agni moves between heaven and earth. The poet requests him to “overflow with strength”. People praise Jātavedas.	
9ab		Agni encompassed the “residences”.
9cd	“We should confirm the observance (of Agni).”	
10ab	The poet desires Vaiśvānara’s abode. (*ā cake.*)	
10c		Agni was born and filled up Heaven and Earth.
10d	Agni encompasses all the world.	
11		“The unique seer” released *bṛhat*. Agni was born.

The two threads, which are concerned with the actual ritual and the cosmogony, respectively, correspond with each other: 4abc (perf.) and 4d (pres.) show the continuity between the cosmogony and the ritual taking place now. Agni encompasses heaven and earth in 9ab (perf.) and 10d (pres.). Further Agni is requested to “overflow with strength” in Verse 7, and this seems to correspond to Verse 11, the release of *bṛhat* by “the unique seer”. I interpret this correspondence as follows: 1) The passages in the perfect tense are flashbacks to the cosmogony, which have been inserted in the context of the ritual taking place now. 2) The ritual taking place is a re-play of the cosmogony. In other words, the poet is carrying out the ritual while remembering the cosmological scenes. He requests Agni to “overflow with strength”, while “the unique seer” released *bṛhat* in the cosmogony. The correspondence between Verse 7 and 11 indicates that “the unique seer” in Verse 11 is Agni Vaiśvānara. Now, in Verse 10, Agni has encompassed all the world, just as he did in the cosmogony. Something which corresponds to the release of *bṛhat* must happen in the next scene in the actual ritual. What is released by Agni Vaiśvānara?

A clue for us might be the motif "Agni's birth" which is mentioned in Verses 10 and 11, which appears to belong to the same Agni myth as the release of *bṛhat*.

As is well known, Agni is said to have threefold births[194]. RV 10.45.1 mentions them in the clearest way:

RV 10.45.1 First, Agni was born from heaven. Jātavedas [was born] from us secondly. Thirdly [he was born] in the waters. Having heroic mind, kindling the perpetual [fire], the heedful [priest] watches over him[195].

Here Agni's births are said to be: 1) from heaven (*divás*), 2) from us (*asmád*), and 3) in the waters (*apsú*) [196]. Among these, the second one

[194] Cf. Oldenberg (1917) pp.106-107, Hillebrandt (1927) p.136.

[195] *divás pári prathamám̐ jajñe agnír asmád dvitī́yam pári jātávedāḥ / tṛtī́yam apsú nṛmáṇā ájasram índhāna enam̐ jarate svādhī́ḥ //*

[196] RV 1.95.3 seems to be somewhat parallel to the above verse: *trī́ṇi jā́nā pári bhūṣanty asya samudrá ékam̐ divy ékam apsú* "They make his three births prosper: one in the heavenly ocean, one in the waters." This passage is ambiguous. Geldner's translation is: "Seine drei Geburten umfassen sie (im Geiste): die eine im Meere, eine im Himmel, (eine?) in den Gewässern". He adds *ékam* to make his translation consistent, but as a result of this addition, his translation contradicts with the statement in RV 10.45.1. If one takes *samudré* and *dívi* as in apposition, he obtains a translation as presented above. The other birth of Agni, which is not mentioned in this verse, is actually mentioned in the preceding verse as the earthly one: 1.95.2 *dáśemám̐ tváṣṭur janayanta gárbham átandrāso yuvatáyo víbhṛtram / tigmā́nīkam̐ sváyaśasam̐ jáneṣu virócamānam pári ṣīm̐ nayanti //* "Ten [fingers] beget this womb of Tvaṣṭṛ. The unwearied young ones [beget] *víbhṛtra*. They lead him around, who has sharp face, who is glorious through his own deeds, who shines among people". But Geldner's translation might be supported by RV 1.163.4, a statement about the birth of a horse: *trī́ṇi ta āhur diví bándhanāni trī́ṇy apsú trī́ṇy antáḥ samudré / utéva me váruṇaś chantsy arvan yátrā ta āhúḥ paramám̐ janítram //* "They say that he has three bindings in heaven, three in the waters, [and] three inside the ocean. And you, o runner, appear to me just like Varuṇa, where they say that his highest birthplace is". This verse is not directly concerned with Agni's birth, but it seems to give *samudré, dívi,* and *apsú* as three different places, and that corresponds well with Geldner's translation of RV 1.95.3. If Geldner is correct, we have two different statements about the threefold birth of Agni. But in any case "heaven" and "the waters" are contained in this statement.

clearly refers to his birth on earth as the sacrificial fire[197]. In the following subsection, we will discuss Agni's birth in heaven.

Agni's birth in the highest heaven

The following verses mention Agni's birth in the highest heaven (*paramé vyòmani*):

RV 1.143.2	Being born in the highest heaven, Agni became manifest for Mātariśvan[198]. When he is kindled by the magical power and greatness, his flame illuminated Heaven and Earth[199].
RV 6.8.2	Being born in the highest heaven, Agni, the lord of obedience, protected the obedience. Vaiśvānara, who has good magical power, measured out the Antarikṣa, and touched the vault with greatness[200].

The following verse mentions "Agni's highest birthplace":

RV 2.9.3	We should offer you at your highest birthplace. O Agni, we should offer with Stomas at your lower seat. I honour the womb from which you have started out. When you are kindled, the oblations have been offered to you[201].

The highest birthplace, which is contrasted with his lower seat, must be, as Geldner claims in his note to this verse, the sun. Pāda b seems to

---

[197] Cf. e.g. RV 5.11.6 *tvā́m agne áṅgiraso gúhā hitám ánv avindañ chiśriyāṇáṃ váne-vane / sá jāyase mathyámānaḥ sáho mahát tvā́m āhuḥ sáhasas putrám aṅgiraḥ //* "O Agni, the Aṅgirases discovered you hidden, abiding in every wood. You are born, when rubbed with mighty strength. They call you the son of strength. O Aṅgiras".

[198] There are two kinds of the statements on Mātariśvan. Some Rigvedic verses say that he comes from the highest heaven, others say that he comes "from afar" (= underworld). However, this does not mean that "the highest heaven" is identical with "the underworld". This point, which seems worth discussing for the consistency, will be discussed in the appendix.

[199] *sá jā́yamānaḥ paramé vyòmany āvír agnír abhavan mātaríśvane / asyá krátvā samidhānásya majmánā prá dyā́vā śocíḥ pṛthivī́ arocayat //*

[200] *sá jā́yamānaḥ paramé vyòmani vratā́ny agnír vratapā́ arakṣata / vy àntárikṣam amimīta sukrátur vaiśvānaró mahinā́ nā́kam aspṛśat //*

[201] *vidhéma te paramé jánmann agne vidhéma stómair ávare sadhásthe / yásmād yóner udā́rithā yáje tám prá tvé havī́ṃṣi juhure sámiddhe //*

support this interpretation: the sacrificial fire on earth is kindled, and the sun in heaven receives the oblations.

Macdonell (1897), based on AV 3.21.1, 3.21.7, 8.1.11 and AitB 7.7.2, identifies this heavenly birth of Agni with the lightning. In contrast, Oldenberg and Hillebrandt connect the heavenly birth with the sun[202]. The discussion of the two latter authorities is persuasive. And at least we can see no Rigvedic passage which identifies the birth of Agni with that of lightning. And especially the above RV 2.9.3 shows that "Agni's highest birthplace" literally denotes "the highest heaven". So we can in any case identify the Agni in heaven with the sun. However, we still do not know what Agni's *birth* in heaven is. At least, we do not know any natural phenomenon which can be associated with it. The sun appears every morning in the eastern horizon, and disappears every evening into the western horizon. Between the sunrise and sunset, we only see the movement of the sun, and nothing which could be called "Agni's birth in the highest heaven".

Let us start again from RV 3.3.11, our verse in question, which runs "Agni, who magnifies the parents, [namely] the rich-in-sperm Heaven and Earth, was born". A similar expression appears in RV 10.45.8:

RV 10.45.8	Looking like a gold plate, he shone forth widely, illuminating the unforgettable life-energy in the splendour.

[202] Oldenberg (1917: 108): "Beim himmlischen Agni kann die Sonne, kann auch der Blitz in Betracht kommen. Der Blitz seinerseits wieder kann wie als himmlisches so auch als dem Wasserreich entstammendes Wesen verstanden werden: seine Heimat ist ja die Wolke. Wir werden aber sehen, daß für die vedische Vorstellung noch außer dem Blitz in ganz anderem Sinne Feuer in allem Wasser, im irdischen wie im himmlischen enthalten ist. Wo nun Himmelsagni und Wasseragni nebeneinander genannt werden, glaube ich im ganzen, daß jener eher als die Sonne, dieser in der eben berührten, vom Blitz verschiedenen Bedeutung zu verstehen ist". Hillebrandt (1927: 136 and 139-141): "Wir finden als Zeugen für sie in der Hauptsache nur Kommentare und spätere Quellen, auf die sich wohl auch Alberunī India 1, 41 stützt; vereinzelt natürlich auch andere Angaben, denn die Inder haben selbstverständlich den Blitz beobachtet und seine feurige Natur erkannt. Die Stellen aber, wo sie ihn zu einer Gottheit erhoben haben, sind gering an Zahl und gehören mehr dem Adbhuta-Ritual als dem regulären Kultus an... Im allgemeinen sehen wir den Blitz als Waffe in der Hand Indra's, Soma's, Bṛhaspati's und andrer... Wenn wir von den mythologischen Wesen wie Indra, Bṛhaspati u.a. absehen und uns an die durchsichtigen Naturerscheinungen selber halten, so steht der Blitz *aśmán, vidyút* in naher Beziehung zur Sonne als deren Waffe... Ferner steht, wie natürlich, der Blitz in naher Beziehung zu Wolke und Regen. Er wird im übrigen sehr verschiedenartig symbolisiert, aber nirgends fällt eine Äusserung etwa wie *agnir vai vajraḥ (vidyut)* oder *devo vai vajraḥ*".

Agni became immortal with the powers, *when Heaven, who has good sperm, begot him*[203].

Note that both of these verses mention sperm: Heaven (and earth) is said to be "rich in sperm" (3.3.11) and "having good sperm" (10.45.8). This might imply that Agni's birth has something to do with Heaven's sperm. And, inasmuch as father Heaven and mother Earth are mentioned, there must be a sexual intercourse, through which the sperm is released. The following RV passage is crucially important to this point:

RV 1.31.3 O Agni, be first manifest for Mātariśvan with the good magical power for Vivasvat. *Heaven and Earth* trembled at the Hotṛ-selection. You became a match for the burden. You sacrificed to the great, o Vasu[204].

RV 1.31.4 O Agni, you caused Heaven to roar for a man. For the benevolent Purūravas, a more benevolent one [caused Heaven to roar]. When you are released at the *parents* with the power, they lead you around forward and again backward[205].

RV 1.31.3 is parallel to RV 1.143.2 "Being born in the highest sky, Agni became visible to Mātariśvan[206]". This can be regarded as mentioning Agni's birth in heaven[207]. As Geldner correctly notes, "the parents" in 1.31.4 are churning-sticks. The fact that Purūravas is mentioned in 1.31.4 also supports his interpretation, because he represents the "male" churning-stick[208]. However, "the parents" also correspond with the "Heaven and Earth" in 1.31.3, which leads us to the observation that two births of Agni are contrasted in this passage: Agni's birth in heaven (through the sexual intercourse between Heaven and Earth) in 1.31.3, and Agni's birth on earth through using the churning sticks (1.31.4). But why are these two births of Agni contrasted with each other?

The answer is hidden in the spatial structure of the cosmic Agni. As discussed in Chapter 1, the cosmic Agni structure consists of the sun, spoke, and the sacrificial fire. When the sun reaches the vault, the total

---

[203] *dṛśānó rukmá urviyā́ vy àdyaud durmárṣam ā́yuḥ śriyé rucānáḥ / agnír amṛ́to abhavad váyobhir yád enaṃ dyaúr janáyat surétāḥ //*

[204] *tvám agne prathamó mātaríśvana āvír bhava sukratūyā́ vivásvate / árejetāṃ ródasī hotṛvū́ryé 'saghnor bhārám áyajo mahó vaso //*

[205] *tvám agne mánave dyā́m avāśayaḥ purūrávase sukṛ́te sukṛ́ttaraḥ / śvātréṇa yát pitrór múcyase páry ā́ tvā pū́rvam anayann ā́param púnaḥ //*

[206] *sá jā́yamānaḥ paramé vyòmany āvír agnír abhavan mātaríśvane*

[207] See note 198.

[208] See Krick (1982) p.203ff.

structure will be as in the following figure, which looks like the churning sticks:

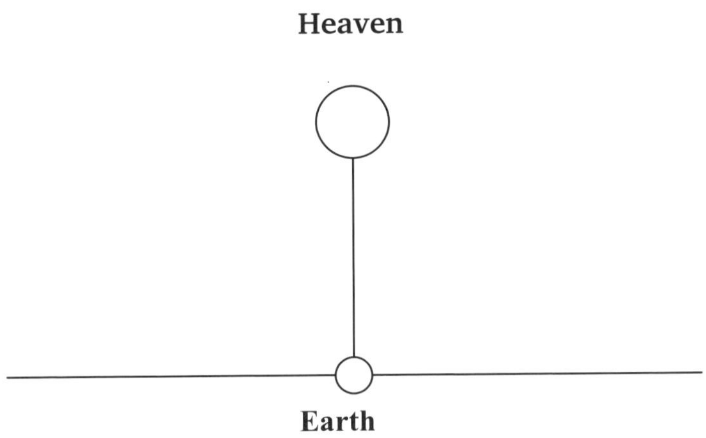

Also, the above figure gives a straight image of sexual intercourse between Heaven and Earth. Namely, Heaven is inserting his penis vertically into Earth.

As has already been seen, sperm is mentioned in some instances of Agni's birth in heaven. If sperm is released as a result of this sexual intercourse, it must be released through the sun, and possibly runs through the spoke towards earth. The reason why this ejaculation is called "Agni's birth" must be that the sperm was conceived as a form of fire. As the figure shows, it is released through the sun[209].

There are at least three Rigvedic passages including RV 3.3, which depicts the scene of Agni's birth in heaven concretely:

RV 7.5.7 *Being born in the highest heaven*, you protect the enclosure around at once, like Vāyu. Producing the creatures, you have roared towards [them], being helpful for the offspring, o Jātavedas[210].

---

[209] As Krick (1982: 189-223) shows, some Brāhmaṇa and Śrautasūtra passages imply the derivation of Agni from heaven, and some of them refer to "Agni's sperm". This point can be explained through the correspondence between Agni's births in heaven and on earth. These two processes have a formal similarity, and they can be likened to each other.

[210] *sá jā́yamānaḥ paramé vyòman vāyúr ná pā́thaḥ pári pāsi sadyáḥ / tvám bhúvanā janáyann abhí krann ápatyāya jātavedo daśayán //*

RV 7.5.8 O Agni Vaiśvānara, Jātavedas, *procure us the bright tonic with which you let overflow the gift*, o procurer of everything, a great fame for the mortal who offers[211].

RV 7.5.9 O Agni, procure the wealth which is rich in cattle and the glorious booty for our patrons. O Agni Vaiśvānara, give a great protection to us, in accordance with Rudras and Vasus[212].

In 7.5.8, Agni is requested to bestow "tonic" (*íṣ*) with which he should "let overflow the gift". From the above discussion, we can assume that Agni's sperm is overflowing here. As Gonda (1989: 177-178) says, "gift" (*rā́dhas*) has a close relation to the success of a ritual[213], and it sometimes comes from a god[214]. In the context of this passage, the word means a gift which is given back from the gods in return for the oblations from the sacrificer.

While the new-born Agni is called Jātavedas in 7.5.7, Agni is called Vaiśvānara as well as Jātavedas in 7.5.8. The releasing Agni is Agni the sun = Agni Vaiśvānara. The released Agni is the Agni which moves between heaven and earth, which must be Agni Jātavedas[215]. At the mo-

---

[211] *tā́m agne asmé íṣam érayasva vaíśvānara dyumátīṃ jātavedaḥ / yáyā rā́dhaḥ pínvasi viśvavāra pṛthú śrávo dāśúṣe mártyāya //*

[212] *táṃ no agne maghávadbhyaḥ purukṣúṃ rayíṃ ní vā́jaṃ śrútyaṃ yuvasva / vaíśvānara máhi naḥ śárma yacha rudrébhir agne vásubhiḥ sajóṣāḥ //*

[213] "However, the above disquisition appears to lead to the conclusion that *rā́dhas* is one of those words ending in the suffix *-as-* which express a potency, power-concept or power-substance, that empirically, or within some form of experience, was supposed to express the idea conveyed by the root *rādh* (the verb *rādhati, rādhnoti*), i.e. "to succeed, to be successful, to complete a task, to accomplish one's purpose", and could therefore denote facts, events, processes, concrete objects which were believed to represent or manifest that idea. Although in principle any manifestation or localization of this power concept could be called *rādhas*, it was in the literature known to us, and as far as we are able to see, especially used to denote those objects or actions which produced, manifested or represented the success of the sacrificial rites and ceremonies such as the *dakṣiṇās* offered to the officiants, including those given to the poets and eulogists inducing the gods to comply with the worshippers' wishes, resulted in the desired effect".

[214] Gonda (1989) p.162ff.

[215] The new-born Agni appears to be called Vaiśvānara in RV 6.8.2 and 3.3.10. However, the invocation of Vaiśvānara in 3.3.10a belongs to the description of the present situation, while 3.3.10cd, which describes Agni's birth, belongs to the description of the cosmogonical situation. 6.8.2ab, which describes Agni's birth, should also be separated from 6.8.2cd, which describes Vaiśvānara's ascent.

ment of the ejaculation, these two are unseparable. That is why Agni is called Vaiśvānara-Jātavedas in 7.5.8. It might be worth noting that 7.5.7cd mentions "producing the creatures" and "being helpful for the offspring". As discussed in chapter 1, Agni Jātavedas is concerned with the procreation of the cattle. It is highly possible that the sperm released here falls down to earth and promotes the propagation of the cattle.

RV 3.2 contains a similar passage:

RV 3.2.10	The human tonics made the seer of the settlements, the chief of the settlements, sharp like an axe. He goes upwards and downwards, while working. *He puts the embryo in these beings*[216].
RV 3.2.11	*The procreating seed bull incites himself into the conspicuous wombs*, while roaring like a lion. Vaiśvānara, who has a wide surface, the immortal one, who distributes the treasure and wealth for a pious one[217].
RV 3.2.12	Vaiśvānara has ascended to heaven as in the ancient time. Being honoured by good hymns, he [ascends] the top of heaven. Producing the wealth for people as before, the watchful one goes round the same course[218].

Agni's birth is mentioned/implied in the preceding verses 3.2.2, 3.2.3, 3.2.7, and 3.2.9[219]. Although it is not explicitly stated that Agni's birth in heaven is described here, the expressions in 3.2.11 that are parallel with RV 3.3 and 7.5[220], and the description of the sun reaching the vault in 3.2.12, make it plausible. Geldner notes to 3.2.10cd: "Wie das irdische Feuer als Material das Brennholz hat, so wird ein solches mystisches auch für die beiden anderen Formen des Agni, für Blitz und Sonne vorausgesetzt." However, the deity who "goes upwards and downwards, while working" must be Agni as Jātavedas, which is also mentioned in

[216] *viśā́ṃ kavíṃ viśpátim mā́nuṣīr íṣaḥ sáṃ sīm akṛṇvan svádhitiṃ ná téjase / sá udváto niváto yāti véviṣat sá gárbham eṣú bhúvaneṣu dīdharat //*

[217] *sá jinvate jaṭháreṣu prajajñivā́n vṛ́ṣā citréṣu nā́nadan ná siṃháḥ / vaiśvānaráḥ pṛthupā́jā ámartyo vásu rátnā dáyamāno ví dāśúṣe //*

[218] *vaiśvānaráḥ pratnáthā nā́kam ā́ruhad divás pṛṣṭhám bhándamānaḥ sumánmabhiḥ / sá pūrvaváj janáyañ jantáve dhánaṃ samānám ájmam páry eti jā́gṛviḥ //*

[219] 3.2.2 *sá rocayaj janúṣā ródasī ubhé*, 3.2.3 *krátvā dákṣasya táruṣo vídharmaṇi devā́so agníṃ janayanta cíttibhiḥ*, 3.2.7 *ā́ ródasī apṛṇad ā́ svàr maháj jātáṃ yád enam apáso ádhārayan*, 3.2.9 *tisró yahvásya samídhaḥ párijmano 'gnér apunann uśíjo ámṛtyavaḥ*.

[220] 3.3.7c *váyāṃsi jinva bṛhatáś ca*, 3.3.1a *vaiśvānarā́ya pṛthupā́jase*, 7.5.8d *pṛthú śrávo dāśúṣe mártyāya*.

3.2.8, and not the lightning. The deity who "incites himself into the shining wombs" can be interpreted as Agni as Vaiśvānara. So, Agni the Sun puts his "embryo" in "these beings" through the movement of Jātavedas. The "conspicuous wombs" in 3.2.11, which seems to denote the same thing as the "beings" in 3.2.10, might be the plants from which the churning sticks are taken[221]. He "incites himself", which seems to mean ejaculation. He is also said to "distribute the treasure and wealth", which corresponds with "gift" (7.5.8) and "glorious booty" (7.5.9).

Let us go back to RV 3.3:

RV 3.3.7	O Agni, be wakeful during the life which has good offspring. *Overflow with strength. Bestow tonic by shining for us. Incite energies and great [vigours].* O watchful one, you are the Uśij of the gods, having good magical powers of the verses.
RV 3.3.10	O Vaiśvānara, I desire your abodes, with which you became the bestower of light, o bright one. *Being born, you filled up the worlds, Heaven and Earth.* O Agni, you encompass all [the worlds] in yourself.
RV 3.3.11	Because of the marvellous powers of Vaiśvānara, *the unique seer released bṛhat with the creative power. Agni, who magnifies the parents, [namely] the rich-in-sperm Heaven and Earth, was born.*

Through the examination of the parallel passages, we can see some implicit associations, which were hidden in the background of the text: Agni Vaiśvānara = the sun = "the unique seer" releases heaven's sperm = *bṛhat* = Agni Jātavedas towards earth, when it reaches the vault. "Agni's birth" mentioned in 3.3.10 is this ejaculation. Just as in the parallel passages, Agni is said to "overflow". As already discussed, this passage is a replay of the cosmogony. The poet requests the sun to release the sperm again for the propagation of the cattle and the fertilization of earth.

From the above discussion, we can support Geldner's interpretation: The *bṛhat* in RV 3.3.11 metaphorically denotes Heaven's sperm, which is released by Agni Vaiśvānara[222].

---

[221] See RV 5.83.1 below.

[222] Oguibenine (1988: 205 and note 41) discusses some passages in which *bṛhat* appears, and indicates their background of verbal contest and distribution of prizes. His observation is correct, but my view is that it does not prevent us from interpreting the present occurrence of *bṛhat* as referring to sperm = light with all the metaphorical associations with released magical speech and cows.

Agni's Landing

RV 3.3, which we studied in the preceding section, is recited in the Third Soma Pressing of the Agniṣṭoma, as the first part of the Āgnimārutaśastra. But what about the relevant non-verbal ritual procedure? Is it implemented with the motif of Agni's ejaculation?

A quite sharp analysis of the Third Soma Pressing is presented by Jamison (1996: 127ff). According to her, this ritual procedure, which takes place in the evening of the Soma pressing day, can be characterized in terms of mixture, and the fertility and procreation as its results. The motif of mixture appears especially in two forms: 1) The mixture of Soma with milk: While the new Soma plant is used in the Morning and Midday Pressings, the dregs left over from the preceding pressings is used in the Third Pressing. This re-pressed Soma juice is mixed with milk and consumed in the ritual. Although the use of dregs might give a somewhat meagre impression, the milk mixture is a well-known theme of many Vedic hymns in which soma juice and milk are considered to be a bull and a cow respectively. In other words, it gives an expression to the notion of fertility. 2) The mixture of the both sexes: the wife of the sacrificer participates in the ritual as one of the most important actors.

The participation of a woman in the ritual, however, causes a considerably heavy structural problem in the implementation of the procedure, because women may in principle not consume Soma, while it is necessary in terms of the total concept of this ritual. The relevant ritual procedure goes as follows: First, the oblation is given to Agni Pātnīvata or the Agni with the wives of the gods. After that, the Agnīdh priest sits on the lap of the Neṣṭṛ priest. Then the Neṣṭṛ fetches the wife of the sacrificer, and he causes her to be looked at by the Udgātṛ priest three times. Then she pours water along her thigh, while a laud called Yajñāyajñīyastotra is sung. After the laud, the Āgnimārutaśastra is recited by the Hotṛ priest.

Jamison's interpretation of this procedure is as follows: Soma (= sperm) is first consumed by the Agnīdh, who takes the female role. Then the Agnīdh takes the male role in turn and transmits the Soma to the Neṣṭṛ, who takes the female role. The Neṣṭṛ now takes the male role, and transmits the Soma to the sacrificer's wife. Here, the procedure is interpreted as the process of the transmission of Soma to the sacrificer's wife, who cannot approach Soma directly because of her female gender. The whole procedure is a sort of conceptual sexual intercourse, where the Udgātṛ functions as the releaser of the sperm. Basically, Soma is dangerous for a woman, and a woman drinking Soma is dangerous for the whole ritual, but in this manner the sacrificer's wife is safely taken into the concept of the ritual.

In fact I believe everything which Jamison writes here. Together with her, we can now precisely trace the logic through which the relevant ritual procedure was implemented. However, I see only one point which she did not fully explain. That is the presence of Agni. She mentions the Pātnīvata offering to Agni and just says "it seems in some ways the equivalent in the Soma Sacrifice of the already examined Patnīsaṃyājas ('joint worship of the wives') that comes toward the end of the ordinary Iṣṭi."[223] I see no further explanation as to why Agni appears here and what his presence means. So this must be our starting point: Why is Agni here at all?

A possible hypothesis in the line of the present study is that it has something to do with the myth of Agni's ejaculation which we discussed above. The following passage in the Taittirīya Brāhmaṇa seems quite important.

TS 6.5.8.3-6 "O drop" he says. The drop is sperm. Thus he impregnates sperm. "Possessing power" he says. Power is offspring. He produces offspring for him. "O Agni" he says. *The impregnator of sperm is Agni.*[224]

Here, Agni is explicitly mentioned as the impregnator. However, quite interestingly, the passage of the Aitareya Brāhmaṇa that explains this Rigvedic recitation tells a story which looks somewhat like that of RV 3.3, but is in fact different from it. The following translation is largely based on Keith's:

AitB 3.33 Prajāpati set his mind on his own daughter. Some say Heaven, others say Uṣas. Having become a stag he approached her in the form of a deer. The gods saw him, "Prajāpati now does a deed unknown". They sought one to punish him; they found him not among one another. They brought together these most dread forms in one place. Brought together they became (*abhavat*) this deity here; therefore his name contains (the word) Bhūta; he who knows thus his name prospers. To him the gods said "Prajāpati here has done a deed unknown. Pierce him." "Yes," he replied, "Let me choose a boon from you." "Choose." He chose this boon, the overlordship of cattle; therefore his name contains the word "cattle". He who knows thus this name of his becomes

[223] Jamison (1996: 133)

[224] *indo íty āha réto vā índū réta evá tád dadhātī́ndriyā́va íty āha prajā́ vā indriyám̐ prajā́ evā́smai prájanayaty agnā3 íty āhāgnír vaí retodhā́ḥ*

rich in cattle. Having aimed at him he pierced him; being pierced he flew upwards; they call him "the deer". The constellation "piercer of the deer" is he. The female deer is the constellation Rohiṇī; the three-pointed arrow is the constellation "three-pointed arrow". The poured seed of Prajāpati ran. It became a pond. The gods said "Let not this seed of Prajāpati be spoiled (*medaṃ* ... *duṣat*)" It became "not to be spoilt" (*māduṣa*). that is why it is called "not to be spoilt". "Connected with man" (*mānuṣa*) is called "not to be spoilt" here, They call "not to be spoilt" mystically "connected with man", for the gods are lovers of mystery as it were.[225]

AitB 3.34 They surrounded it with Agni. The Maruts blew upon it. Agni could not make it move. They surrounded it with Agni Vaiśvānara; the Maruts blew upon it. Then Agni Vaiśvānara caused it to move. The first part of the seed that was kindled up became yonder Āditya. The second became Bhṛgu. Varuṇa took him. Therefore Bhṛgu is Varuṇic. The third (part), that was brilliant as it were, became the Ādityas. The coals became the Aṅgirases. In that the coals after being quenched blazed forth again, Bṛhaspati came into being. The extinguished coals became black cattle. The reddened earth ruddy (cattle). The ash which there was crept about in diverse forms,

[225] *prajāpatir vai svāṃ duhitaram abhyadhyāyad divam ity anya āhur uṣasam ity anye / tām ṛśyo bhūtvā rohitam bhūtām abhyait / taṃ devā apaśyann akṛtaṃ vai prajāpatiḥ karotīti / te tam aichan ya enam āriṣyaty etam anyonyasmin nāvindaṃs / teṣāṃ yā eva ghoratamās tanva āsaṃs tā ekadhā samabharaṃs / tāḥ sambhṛtā eṣa devo 'bhavat tad asyaitad bhūtavan nāma / bhavati vai sa yo 'syaitad evaṃ nāma veda / taṃ devā abruvann ayaṃ vai prajāpatir akṛtam akar imaṃ vidhyeti / sa tathety abravīt sa vai vo varaṃ vṛṇā iti / vṛṇīṣveti / sa etam eva varam avṛṇīta paśūnām ādhipatyaṃ / tad asyaitat paśuman nāma / paśumān bhavati yo 'syai tad evaṃ nāma veda / tam abhyāyatyāvidhyat sa viddha ūrdhva udaprapatat tam etaṃ mṛga ity ācakṣate / ya u eva mṛgavyādhaḥ sa u eva sa yā rohit sā rohiṇī yo eveṣus trikāṃḍā so eveṣus trikāṃḍā / tad vā idaṃ prajāpate retaḥ siktam adhāvat tat saro 'bhavat / te devā abruvan medaṃ prajāpate reto duṣad iti / yad abruvan medaṃ prajāpate reto duṣad iti tan māduṣam abhavat tan māduṣasya māduṣatvaṃ / māduṣaṃ ha vai nāmaitad yan mānuṣaṃ tan māduṣaṃ san mānuṣam ity ācakṣate parokṣeṇa parokṣapriyā iva hi devāḥ*

> the buffalo, the Gayal, the antelope, the camel, the ass, and these ruddy animals.[226]

Our question is whether this story is connected to our myth of Agni's ejaculation in RV 3.3.

It is in fact difficult to show that the incest myth is related to Agni's ejaculation. On the other hand, it is also difficult to say that they are not connected with each other. I present two Rigvedic versions of this incest myth to discuss this point[227].

RV 1.71.5	When he (Agni?) makes the juice for the great father Heaven, he (the shooter), having noticed the gentle females, goes down. The shooter releases missile at him boldly. The god puts the glare on his own daughter[228].
RV 1.71.8	When the heat attains to the lord of men to release, pure sperm is poured down. Heaven [discharges it] at the contact. Agni begets an irreproachable, young, well-minded troop (the Aṅgirases), and makes them complete[229].

The following translation is borrowed from Jamison (1991: 294ff) with a minor change of terms.

---

[226] *tad agninā paryādadhus tan maruto dhūnvaṃs tad agnir na prācyāvayat / tad agninā vaśvānareṇa paryādadhus tan maruto dūnvaṃs tad agnir vaiśvānaraḥ prācyāvayat / tasya yad retasaḥ prathamam udadīpyata tad asāv ādityo 'bhavad / yad dvitīyam āsat tad bhṛgur abhavat / taṃ varuṇo nyagṛṇhīta tasmāt sa bhṛgur vāruṇir / atha yat tṛtīyam adīded iva ta ādityā abhavan / ye 'ṅgārā āsaṃs te 'ṅgiraso 'bhavan / yad aṅgārāḥ punar avaśāntā udadīpyanta tad bṛhaspatir abhavad / yāni parikṣāṇāny āsaṃs te kṛṣṇāḥ paśavo 'bhavan yā lohinī mṛttikā te rohitā / atha yad bhasmāsīt tat paruṣyaṃ vyasarpad gauro gavaya ṛśya uṣṭro gardabha iti ye caite 'ruṇāḥ paśavas /*

[227] Oldenberg Noten also mentions RV 3.31, but it is quite doubtful that it has continuity with 1.71 and 10.61. The suspected offender is called "conveyor" (*váhni*) in 3.31.1, but according to our research in Chapter 1 this cannot be the sun or Heaven, but Agni Jātavedas. It is also not certain that incest is really happening here. I suspect that this verse might show a very early form of the incest myth, but there is not enough material to discuss it. Jamison (1991) does not mention 3.31 either.

[228] *mahé yát pitrá īṃ rásaṃ divé kár áva tsarat pṛśanyàś cikitvā́n / sṛjád ástā dhṛṣatā́ didyúm asmai svā́yāṃ devó duhitári tvíṣiṃ dhāt.*

[229] *ā́ yád iṣé nṛpátiṃ téja ā́naṭ chúci réto níṣiktaṃ dyaúr abhī́ke / agníḥ śárdham anavadyáṃ yúvānaṃ svādhyàṃ janayat sūdáyac ca.*

RV 10.61.5 [The one] whose [penis, which] performs the manly work, stretched out, discharging [the sperm] — that one, the manly one, then pulled away [his penis, which had been] attending on [her]. He tore out again from the maiden, his daughter, what [had been] thrust in — he the unmastered[230].

RV 10.61.7 When the father sprang upon his own daughter, uniting [with her], *he poured down sperm upon the earth*. The gods of good thought engendered the formulation and fashioned [from it] Vāstoṣpati, the protector of the commandments[231].

The offender is Heaven according to 1.71.5. In 10.61.7, Earth as the receiver of the sperm is mentioned. So the sperm released from Heaven falls on Earth. It might be possible to assume continuity between the incest myth and Agni's ejaculation based on this point. However, RV 3.3 and other instances discussed in the previous section do not attest it. Therefore it is also possible to assume that Agni's ejaculation in RV 3.3 was not caused by the incest. It seems me proper to treat these two motifs as two independent myths without excluding the possibility that they are possibly connected to each other.

There are four major versions of the incest myth in Brāhmaṇas. ŚB 1.7.4, MS 4.2.12, JB 3.262-264, and AitB 3.33, which has already been mentioned above[232]. The MS version runs as follows:

MS 4.2.12 Prajāpati created three great [deities]: Agni, Vāyu, and Sūrya. These four, the father and sons, carried out a Sattra. They sprinkled down the sweat together. He came into being. So, this became his name, "he has come into being (*abhūt*)", "[this] all has come into being (*sarvam abhūt*)". So, these two names of him are cruel and unappeased. Therefore, these [names] should not be seized, because they are cruel and unappeased. Prajāpati desired his own daughter Uṣas. She became a deer. He became a stag and went over her. It seemed to be a transgression to him (Rudra). He turned toward

---

[230] *práthiṣṭa yásya vīrákarmam iṣṇád ánuṣṭhitaṃ nú náryo ápauhat / púnas tád ā́ vṛhati yát kanā́yā duhitúr ā́ ánubhṛtam anarvā́ //*

[231]*pitā́ yát svā́ṃ duhitáram adhiṣkán kṣmayā́ rétaḥ saṃjagmānó ní ṣiñcat / svādhyò 'janayan bráhma devā́ vā́stoṣ pátiṃ vratapā́ṃ nír atakṣan.*

[232] Besides these, there are fragmental versions: ŚB 6.1.3.8, PB 8.2.10, ŚB 2.1.2.9, TB 3.1.4.2.

> him with an outstretched [arrow][233]. He (Prajāpati) was afraid of him. He said, "I make you the lord of the cattle (*paśūnāṃ ... pati*). So do not throw [it] to me." So, this [became] his name: "Paśupati". He (Rudra) approached him, and pierced him. He (Rudra) roared (*arodīt*). So, this [became] his name: "Rudra". These two names of him are auspicious and appeased. Therefore, these [names] can be seized at will, because these are auspicious and appeased. The sperm, which first fell away from him, they set it to flames from all sides with Agni. This is why they (cows) are called "Aghnyā". What ran beyond from him, Bṛhaspati caught it. This is why they (cows) are called "Usriyā". [They said,] "We have succeeded". This is why they (cows) are called "Śakvarī". They said "We have come to know how to go." This is why they are called "Go". These are their (cow's) names. He who knows thus enjoys all their names, all the pleasures.[234]

There are several important motifs here. First I would like to compare them with those of the AitB version.

	AitB	MS
Prajāpati (or Heaven)'s incest with his daughter	○	○
The gods search for someone to punish him	○	
Creation of Rudra by gods	○	○
Explanation of Rudra's epithets	○	○

---

[233] I follow Jamison (1991: 291).

[234] *prajā́patir vaí trī́n mahimnò 'sṛjatāgníṁ vāyúṁ sū́ryaṃ / té catvā́raḥ pitāputrā́ḥ sattrám āsata / té svédaṁ samávaukṣaṁs / tád ábhavat* (*abhavat*? Cf. Mittwede 1986) */ tád vā́ asyaitán nā́mābhūt íti / sárvam abhūd íti / tád vā́ asyaité nā́manī krūré áśānte / tásmād eté ná grahītavyè / krūré 3hy eté áśānte / prajā́patir vaí svā́ṃ duhitáram abhyàkāmayatoṣásaṁ / sā́ rohíd abhavat / tā́m ṛ́śyo bhūtvā́dhyait / tásmā ápavratam achadayat / tám ā́yatayābhiparyā́vartata / tásmād vā́ abibhet* (Cf. Mittwede 1986) */ sò 'bravīt / paśūnā́ṃ tvā pátiṃ karomy / átha me mā́sthā* (Cf Mittwede 1986) *íti / tád vā́ asyaitán nā́ma paśupátir íti / tám abhyāyátyāvidhyat / sò 'rodīt / tád vā́ asyaitán nā́ma rudrá íti / té vā́ asyaité nā́manī śivé śānté / tásmād eté kā́mamṃ grahītavyè / śivé 3hy eté śānté / táto yát prathamáṁ rétaḥ parā́patat tád agnínā páryainddha / tád āsām aghnyātvám̩ / táto yád atyásravat tád bṛ́haspátir úpāgṛhṇāt / tád āsām usriyātvám / áśakāméti / tád āsāṁ śakvarītvám̩ / gātúm avidāméti / tád āsāṃ gotvám / etā́ni vā́ āsāṃ nā́māni / sárvair evā́sāṃ nāmabhiḥ sárvaiḥ kā́mair bhuṅkte yá eváṁ véda /*

Rudra's punishment of Prajāpati/Heaven	○	○
Prajāpati's ascent and Explanation of the constellations	○	
Prajāpati's ejaculation	○	○
Sperm becomes pond *mānuṣa*	○	
Creation of various animals	○	

Although this is a rough comparison, it is clear that some of the motifs are lacking in MS. And when we compare the MS version with the Rigvedic versions, it is noticeable that the motifs contained in the MS version are contained in either of the Rigvedic versions, except the explanation of Rudra's epithets, which are typical to Brāhmaṇas. So it seems reasonable to conclude that the MS version presents a more original form of the story.

Here, I would like to mention another study by Stephanie Jamison, which might show us how far we have come. The incest myth was put in the context of the Svarbhānu myth by Jamison (1991), who concludes that together they formed a single myth-complex. According to her, the total story is as follows: The sun committed incest against his daughter Uṣas. Agni, in his fierce aspect as Rudra and bearing the epithet Svarbhānu, punished the sun. Agni pierced the sun with the darkness. The wound remained on the sun's surface as sunspots, and he was covered with smoke. The sunspots transformed into the plants on earth and the smoke was removed in the same manner as embryo covers from a newborn[235]. As Jamison further discusses, the Svarbhānu myth is often associated with the Gavāmayana ritual, and it is typically told in connection with its Viṣuvant Day. And in that case it is rather natural for us to think that the incest myth was also originally told in connection with the Gavāmayana, and that it was later imported to the context of the Third Soma Pressing, concretely, from MS 4.2.12 to AitB 3.33.

When we think in this way, it is highly probable that the additional motifs such as the creation of animals represent the original context of AitB. A striking motif is Agni Vaiśvānara in the creation of various animals. It shows in any case the presence of fire in the scene. The passage of the creation presents a clear image of burning sperm, which produces various creatures. And this comes very close to the concept of Agni's descent[236]. Remember that the releaser of the sperm was Heaven in the

---

[235] Jamison (1991) pp.302-303

[236] There is one more thing in this passage which might also possibly be associated to Agni. That is the name of the pond *mānuṣa*. As Caland (1914: 90) mentions, the place-name *mānuṣa* appears in AV 20.128.12 and JB 3.245, and so it certainly denotes a place here. However Agni is called *mānuṣa* in RV 3.9.6: *tám tvā mártā agr̥bhṇata devébhyo havyavāhana / víśvān*

Rigvedic version of the incest myth, and this original offender is also suggested in AitB. This will lead us to a clear understanding of the story: Prajāpati=Heaven releases sperm, and it falls as fertile fire. In other words, the imported incest myth was put in the context of Agni's descent. The Aitareyins understood this incest myth as a story of descent of Agni, while the Maitrāyaṇīyas possibly did not.

Two other Brāhmaṇa versions of the incest myth should still be mentioned.

The ŚB version of the incest myth is concerned with the elucidation of the fore-portion of the Full- and New-Moon Sacrifices. It explains that the fore-portion was originally a part of the main sacrifice, and that it was cut out from Prajāpati, who symbolizes sacrifice, by Rudra. However, ŚB 1.7.4.4 mentions that name of the Āgnimārutaśastra, and this means the writer of the ŚB version knew the AitB version, because the Āgnimārutaśastra is outside the context of the New- and Full-Moon sacrifices, and the only incest myth which takes place in the context of the Āgnimārutaśastra is that of AitB. It is likely that he made use of the AitB version, and made a new branch of the story.

The JB version looks very much like the AitB version. The following translation is largely based on Caland's[237], and partly on Jamison (1991: 292):

JB 3.262	The Gods, undertaking a sacrificial session, said: "What of us is horrid, that we will produce, in order not to undertake the sacrifice with (that) horrid (part)." What was horrid of them that they produced, and cleansing it, put it down on (between) two earthen plates, thereupon they undertook the sacrificial session. Therefrom the not-wicked God was born. Because he was born out of the plates, that is his name. It was Agni that here was born. He who knows this is not hurt by this [god]. He said to the gods: "For what have ye caused me to come into existence?" "For carefully watching," they replied, "Thou shalt kill him who may transgress." Now, Prajāpati had set his mind on his own daughter, the Dawn. She, having become a red deer, stood for him. He, having become a spotted deer, leaped on her. He saw, "For this did the gods create me, for carefully watching. This one transgresses. Well, I will pierce him."

yád yajñā́m̐ abhipā́si mānuṣa táva krátvā yaviṣṭhya // The pond *mānuṣa* is the sperm of Prajāpati/Heaven, and when it burns it produces coals. It can be a pun.

[237] Cf. his note on PB 8.2.10.

He pierced. He (Prajāpati), pierced, having thrown away this form, and went upward.[238]

JB 3.263 This (arrow shot by Rudra) is (the constellation called) "the three-knotted arrow". For this reason, a spotted one is the most distasteful. And for this reason, he laments, so to say. After he (Prajāpati) was shot, his seed fell down and came down on the Himavat. It became *mānuṣa*. About this the Gods and the Seers, coming together, said: "Let not this be spoiled". Because they had said "let it not be spoiled" (*medaṃ duṣat*), hence it was *māduṣam*, and *māduṣam* is called *mānuṣam*. They set it to flames on all sides by Agni, the Maruts blew on it, by means of the śrāyantīya they strengthened it (*aśrīṇan*): hence the name *śrāyantīya*. Therefrom animals were born. Those (animals) that first came into existence are the red ones; those that came into existence out of the (seed) when it was being heated, are the reddish brown ones; those that came into existence out of the (seed) when it was heated, are the brown ones; those that came into existence out of the (seed), when it was being burned, are the white and the black (animals), and therefore, this same fire burns the white as well as the black (animal); out of the sparks were created the goats and the antelopes; out of the coals the Aṅgirases.[239]

---

[238] *devā vai satram upayanto 'bruvan — yan naḥ krūram ātmanas tan nirmimāmahai / mā sakrūrā upagāmeti / tad yad eṣāṃ krūram ātmana āsīt tan nirmāya śarāvayos saṃmārjaṃ nyadadhuḥ / atha satram upāyan / tata eṣo 'khalo devo 'jāyata / tad yac charāvābhyām ajāyata tad asyaitan nāma / eṣa ha vāva so 'gnir jajñe / na hainam eṣa hinasti ya evaṃ veda / sa devān abravīt — kasmai mām ajījanateti / aupadraṣṭryāyety abruvan — yo 'tipādayāt taṃ hanāsā iti / prajāpatir hoṣasaṃ svāṃ duhitaram abhyadhyāyat / sāsmai rohid bhūtvātiṣṭhat / tāṃ pṛṣato bhūtvāskandat / sa aikṣatāsmai vai māṃ devā ajījanann aupadraṣṭryāya / ati vā ayaṃ pādayati hantainaṃ vidhyānīti / tam avidhyat / sa viddha etad rūpaṃ pratyasyordhva udakrāmat //*

[239] *sa eṣa iṣus trikāṇḍaḥ / tasmāt pṛṣato 'svādutamaḥ / tasmād u śocatīva / tasya viddhasya retaḥ parāpatat / tad dhimavati pratyatiṣṭhat / tan mānuṣam abhavat / tad devāś carṣayaś copasametyābruvan — medaṃ duṣad iti / yad abruvan — medaṃ duṣad iti tan māduṣasya māduṣatvam / māduṣaṃ ha vai nāmaitat / tan mānuṣam ity ākhyāyate / tad agninā paryaindhata / maruto 'dhaman / śrāyantīyenainad aśrīṇan / tac chrāyantīyasya śrāyantīyatvam / tataḥ paśavo 'sṛjyanta / ye prathame 'sṛjyanta te rohināḥ / ye 'bhitapyamānād asṛjyanta te 'ruṇāḥ / ye 'bhitaptād asṛjyanta te babhravaḥ / ye dahyamānād*

JB 3.264 Out of the ashes mixed with coals were created the three cows: the one dedicated to Mitra and Varuṇa, the one dedicated to Bṛhaspati and the one dedicated to the All-Gods; out of the ashes the donkey was created; therefore he is (in colour) the counterpart of the ashes; therefore he lives being unsteady[240].[241]

The motif of the burning sperm is also visible here. However, I do not know whether it makes sense in the given context, and I suppose that this text was copied from AitB into JB together with the knowledge of the descent of Agni. This point will further be discussed in Chapter 3.

As a result of the above discussion, we can understand that the relevant ritual procedure was constructed with the concept of Agni's descent, in which Agni, born in the highest heaven, falls down to earth as sperm. When the development of the ritual required the participation of a woman as the receptacle of the sperm, the priests' apparently ridiculous performances were formed. The Third Soma Pressing is not a plain fertility ritual. A female participant would not have been necessary, if the Third Soma Pressing had been a normal fertility ritual. You could just pray for rain to the father heaven. What is coming down here from heaven is not rain, but sperm of the sun as the fertile fire. Therefore you absolutely need a woman who receives it in her body and fertilizes our world. An essentially important work which no man can ever achieve.

In this chapter, we treated the myth of the ejaculation of fire which forms the background of the Third Soma Pressing. The above discussion corresponds to the point indicated by the arrow in the concept scheme below.

asṛjyanta te śvetāś ca kṛṣṇāś ca / tasmād v ayam evāgnir dahati śvetaṃ caiva kṛṣṇaṃ ca / viṣphuliṃgābhya evājāś caiṇayāś cāsṛjyanta aṅgārebhyo 'ṅgirasaḥ //

240 Caland "being ridden". I conjecture *babhramāṇo* instead of *babhriyamāṇo*.

241 *aṅgāramiśrād bhasmanas tisro vaśā asṛjyanta — maitrāvaruṇī bārhaspatyā vaiśvadevī / bhasmana eva gardabho 'sṛjyata / tasmāt sa bhasmanaḥ pratirūpaḥ / tasmāt sa babhriyamāṇo jīvati /*

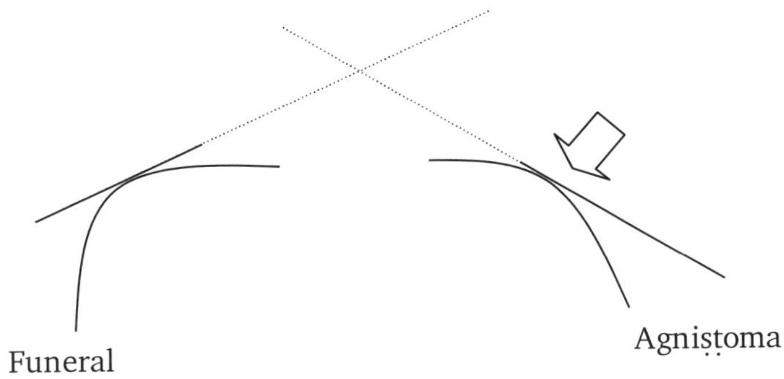
Funeral
Agniṣṭoma

Chapter 3: Circulation of Fire

The *pañcāgnividyā*, or the teaching of five fires, is an old Indian theory which explains the derivation of an individual. According to Oberlies (1998: 478ff), it replaced a Rigvedic concept of reincarnation in which a deceased person is born again in the same family as an offspring of himself. Oberlies and Wilden (2000: 189ff) think that this theory essentially represents a circulation of water. I certainly admit that this concept underlies the *pañcāgnividyā*, but it does not explain all the details. I would like to discuss the formation of the Jaiminīya Brāhmaṇa version of the *pañcāgnividyā* to make this point clear.

The *pañcāgnividyā* is transmitted in JB 1.45, ChU 5.4.1ff, and BĀU 6.2.9ff. Apart from these, we have ŚB 11.6.2.6ff, which has considerable similarity with them. Schmithausen (1994) showed that the Upaniṣad versions can be understood as adaptations of the JB version with ŚB 11.6.2 as a model, and this observation can be our starting point. In other words, the Upaniṣad versions are less relevant for our discussion about the prehistory of the *pancāgnividyā*. According to Wilden (2000) the JB version can be derived from ŚB 11.6.2 via the version *X which has not been transmitted. My first question is whether Wilden's idea is valid.

I would like to present the translations of the relevant passages just for the ease of our discussion. I borrow the translation of JB 1.45 from Bodewitz (1973).

JB 1.45	The one that shines here (the sun), that is Agni Vaiśvānara. Its fuel is the night, its flame the day, its smoke the rays of the sun, its sparks the stars, its coals the moon. In this same Agni Vaiśvānara the gods day by day offer immortality, the (heavenly) waters. From this oblation when it has been offered King Soma comes into existence.[242] The thunder is Agni Vaiśvānara. Its fuel is heaven, its flame the lightning, its smoke the clouds, its sparks the hailstones, its coals the thunderbolt. In this same Agni Vaiśvānara the gods day by day offer King Soma.

[242] *eṣa vā agnir vaiśvānaro ya eṣa tapati / tasya rātris samid ahar jyotī raśmayo dhūmo nakṣatrāṇi visphuliṅgāś candramā aṅgārāḥ / tasminn etasminn agnau vaiśvānare 'harahar devā amṛtam apo juhvati / tasyā āhuter hutāyai somo rājā saṃbhavati //*

From this oblation when it has been offered rain comes into existence.[243]

The earth is Agni Vaiśvānara. Its fuel is the atmosphere, its flame the fire, its smoke the wind, its sparks the shining motes in the air, its coals the quarters. In this same Agni Vaiśvānara the gods day by day offer rain. From this oblation when it has been offered food comes into existence.[244]

Man is Agni Vaiśvānara. Its fuel is speech, its flame sight, its smoke breath, its sparks mind, its coals hearing. In this same Agni Vaiśvānara the gods day by day offer food. From this oblation when it has been offered seed comes into existence.[245]

Woman is Agni Vaiśvānara. Its fuel is the vagina, its flame the vulva, its smoke desire, its sparks the feelings of enjoyment, its coals the coitus. In this same Agni Vaiśvānara the gods day by day offer seed. From this oblation when it has been offered man comes into existence.[246]

Thus in this fifth creation man is born from the gods. At the fifth creation the divine waters speak with a human voice.[247]

ŚB 11.6.2.6ff Well, these two libations, after having been offered, rise upwards. They enter the atmosphere, and make the atmosphere an Āhavanīya fire, the wind the fuel, the

---

[243] *stanayitnur evāgnir vaiśvānaraḥ / tasya dyaus samid vidyuj jyotir abhrāṇi dhūmo hlādanayo viṣphuliṅgā aśanir aṅgārāḥ / tasminn etasminn agnau vaiśvānare 'harahar devās somaṃ rājānaṃ juhvati / tasyā āhuter hutāyai vṛṣṭis saṃbhavati //*

[244] *pṛthivy evāgnir vaiśvānaraḥ / tasyāntarikṣaṃ samid agnir jyotir vāyur dhūmo marīcayo viṣphuliṅgā diśo 'ṅgārāḥ / tasminn etasminn agnau vaiśvānare 'harahar devā vṛṣṭiṃ juhvati / tasyā āhuter hutāyā annaṃ saṃbhavati*

[245] *puruṣa evāgnir vaiśvānaraḥ / tasya vāk samic caksur jyotiḥ prāṇo dhūmo mano viṣphuliṅgāś śrotram aṅgārāḥ / tasminn etasminn agnau vaiśvānare 'harahar devā annaṃ juhvati / tasyā āhuter hutāyai retas saṃbhavati //*

[246] *striyo vā agnir vaiśvānaraḥ / tasyopasthaṃ samid yonir jyotir iṣyā dhūmo 'bhinando viṣphuliṅgās saṃsparśo 'ṅgārāḥ / tasminn etasminn agnau vaiśvānare 'harahar devā reto juhvati / tasyā āhuter hutāyai puruṣas saṃbhavati //*

[247] *so 'tra pañcamyāṃ visṛṣṭyāṃ puruṣo devebhyo jāyate / pañcamyāṃ visṛṣṭyāṃ divyā āpaḥ puruṣavāco vadanti //*

sun-motes the pure libation: they satisfy the atmosphere, and go out from there.[248]

They enter heaven, and make heaven an Āhavanīya fire, the sun the fuel, and the moon the pure libation: they satisfy heaven, and return from there.[249]

They enter this [earth], and make this [earth] an Āhavanīya fire, the fire the fuel, and the herbs the pure libation: they satisfy this [earth], and go out from there.[250]

They enter man, and make his mouth an Āhavanīya fire, his tongue the fuel, and food the pure libation: they satisfy man; and, He who, knowing thus, eats food, by him the Agnihotra is offered. They go out from there.[251]

They enter woman, and make her vagina an Āhavanīya, her womb the fuel, — for that (womb) is called the bearer, because by it Prajāpati bore creatures, — and the sperm the pure libation: they satisfy woman. He who, knowing thus, has sexual intercourse, by him the Agnihotra is offered. The son who is born therefrom is the renascent world: this is the Agnihotra, Yājñavalkya, there is nothing higher than this.[252]

I present a partial table of comparison below, following Schmithausen.

		Offering fire	Fuel	Oblation	Result
1	JB ŚB	*ya eṣa tapati* (a/b) *div-*	*rātri-* *āditya-*	*amṛtam āpas* *candramās*	*somo rājā* —

[248] *té vā́ eté ā́hutī huté útkrāmataḥ té antárikṣam ā́viśatas té antárikṣam évāhavanī́yaṃ kurvā́te vāyúṃ samídhaṃ márīcīr evá śukrā́m ā́hutiṃ té antárikṣaṃ tarpayatas té táta útkrāmataḥ //*

[249] *té dívam ā́viśataḥ té dívam évāhavanī́yaṃ kurvā́te ādityáṃ samídhaṃ candrámasam evá śukrā́m ā́hutiṃ té dívaṃ tarpayatas té táta ā́vartete //*

[250] *té imā́m ā́viśataḥ té imā́m évāhavanī́yaṃ kurvā́te agníṃ samídham óṣadhīr evá śukrā́m ā́hutiṃ té imā́ṃ tarpayatas té táta útkrāmataḥ //*

[251] *té púruṣam ā́viśataḥ tásya múkham évāhavanī́yaṃ kurvā́te jihvā́ṃ samídham ánnam evá śukrā́m ā́hutiṃ té púruṣaṃ tarpayataḥ sá yá eváṃ vidvā́n aśnā́ty agnihoyrám évāsya hutáṃ bhavati té táta útkrmataḥ //*

[252] *té stríyam ā́viśataḥ tásyā upástham évāhavanī́yaṃ kurvā́te dhā́rakāṃ samídhaṃ dhā́rakā ha vaí nā́maíṣaitáyā ha vaí prajāpatiḥ prajā́ dhārayā́ṃ cakāra réta evá śukrā́m ā́hutiṃ té stríyaṃ tarpayataḥ sá yá eváṃ vidvā́n mithunám upaíty agnihotrám évāsya hutáṃ bhavati yás tátaḥ putró jā́yate sá lokáḥ pratyutthā́yy etád agnihotráṃ yājñavalkya nā́taḥ páram asti*

2	JB ŚB	*stanayitnu-* (a/b) *antarikṣa-*	*div-* *vāyu-*	*somo rājā* *marīcayas*	*vṛṣṭi-* —
3	JB ŚB	*pṛthivī-* (a/b) *iyam*	*antarikṣa-* *agni-*	*vṛṣṭi-* *oṣadhayas*	*anna-* —
4	JB ŚB	*puruṣa-* (a)*puruṣa-* (b)*mukha-*	*vāc-* *jihvā-*	*anna-* *anna-*	*retas* —
5	JB ŚB	*strī* (a)*strī* (b)*upastha-*	*upastham* *dhārakā*	*retas* *retas*	*puruṣa-* *putra-*

The actual order of ŚB is 2-1-3-4-5, which is changed here for the comparison of the elements. In ŚB the region reached (a) and the offering fire (b) are differentiated.

When we compare JB and ŚB, it is quite noticeable that the JB version is far less consistent in terms of the cosmological structure. While ŚB consistently follows the normal tripartite structure of heaven, atmosphere and earth in the first three dimensions, JB has heaven in the fuel of the second dimension which seems to represent atmosphere, and atmosphere in the fuel of the third dimension which represents earth. This seems to be the starting point for Wilden, who derives the *pañcāgnividyā* of JB from ŚB 11.6.2. Although her discussion is quite difficult to follow, she apparently distinguishes the upper half of the atmosphere from the lower half, and tries to explain the "heaven" in the fuel of the second dimension and the "atmosphere" in the fuel of the third dimension as a result of this special cosmology. In other words, the upper side of the atmosphere touches heaven, and that is the reason why the "heaven" appears in the second dimension. In the same manner, the lower side of the atmosphere touches earth, and earth and the lower atmosphere are integrated into the third dimension[253]. However, besides being too artificial, it leaves some quite important points unexplained.

First, the JB version of the *pañcāgnividyā* and ŚB 11.6.2 are based on different total concepts. In JB, the output of the dimension n is always the input of the dimension $n+1$. So, when we write the relevant operation "f_n", we can write its total concept as follows with high school mathematics.

$$f_5(f_4(f_3(f_2(f_1(\text{the heavenly waters}))))) = \text{man}$$

In contrast, the successive actions in ŚB are not related to each other in this way. They can only be written as separate actions:

[253] Wilden (2000) pp.196-198.

f_1(the two libations)
f_2(the two libations)
f_3(the two libations)
f_4(the two libations)
f_5(the two libations) = son

The scheme of JB obviously tells us the origin of the sperm and the new born child in heaven, while it is not explicitly supported by the architecture of ŚB 11.6.2. A preceding step may prepare the environment for the following step, as the sperm implicitly expected as an extra input for the fifth dimension, but each dimension is in principle separated. So, while JB guarantees the identity of the heavenly waters with the sperm, what ŚB shows is the consistency of the Agnihotra libations in all the dimensions, and the production of sperm is one of the results of the libations. This architectural difference suggests that the JB version cannot be simply and linearly derived from ŚB 11.6.2.

Secondly, I see in fact no motive which caused the migration from the consistent structure of ŚB to the apparently illogical arrangement in JB. According to Wilden, this change was triggered by the fact that the meaning of the moon mentioned in ŚB 11.6.2 as the oblation of the highest dimension was not recognized by the people outside the Vājasaneyins' tradition[254]. As she showed quite clearly, the participation of the moon in the circulation of water is peculiar to the ŚB[255]. However, if the improvement of intelligibility were the motive, we would have to say that the JB version is a complete failure, because it presupposes, according to Wilden, a special cosmology which can be observed nowhere else in the Vedic corps. So in any case we have a good reason to assume that the JB version is not a result of the changes which were motivated by the improvement of the intelligibility.

I would like to present an alternative explanation concerning the development of the JB version. I think that we can explain the anomalies of the JB with only restricted influence from ŚB 11.6.2. What we presuppose is the existence of the following statements in the Jaiminīya tradition preceding the formation of the *pañcāgnividyā*.

King Soma	in heaven	becomes rain	through thunder
Rain	in atmosphere	becomes food	through earth
Food	on earth	becomes sperm	through man
Sperm	in man	becomes his son	through woman

254 Wilden (2000) pp.195-196.
255 Wilden (2000) pp.93-94.

This is in fact quite similar to the scheme of the JB in the above partial table except for the first fire. The first column in this proto-*pañcāgnividyā* represents the oblation in the JB version, the second column the fuel, the third column the result, and the fourth column the offering fire. It is noteworthy that this represents a pure teaching of water without any fire element.

The above scheme looks consistent in terms of the cosmological structure. However, suppose the narrative style has changed and we have the following scheme.

Thunder changes	King Soma	of heaven	to rain.
Earth changes	rain	of atmosphere	to food.
Man changes	food	of earth	to sperm.
Woman changes	sperm	of man	to his son.

This scheme looks deficient, because it starts from the atmospheric element "thunder" and not from a heavenly element. The most typical heavenly element is the sun. So let us add it as the first row in the table:

Sun changes	X	of Y	to King Soma.

Although X and Y are not yet filled, we should consider what this addition meant. When this row is added, we have a successive line from the sun to the sperm. As a natural association, the inventor of the *pañcāgnividyā* must have remembered the myth of Agni's descent. It is even not imaginable that he did not, because the myth appears in the same Jaiminīya Brāhmaṇa, as we discussed in Chapter 2[256]. The association led him to a new perspective. The scheme now does not represent a pure water doctrine anymore, because a fire doctrine has become fused with the original water doctrine. He decided to reorganize the scheme by identifying each column with an element of the sacrificial fire. It seems possible that he took ŚB 11.6.2 or its unknown prototype as a model at this point. Thus the sun, thunder, earth, man and woman were put under the header "offering fire". X, King Soma, rain, food and sperm were put under "oblation". Y, heaven, atmosphere, earth and man were put under "fuel", but the "earth" and "man" in this column were adapted to "speech" and "vagina" respectively, seemingly under the influence from the ŚB. As to the addition of the four other columns, namely flame, smoke, sparks

[256] This means either that the author of the *pañcāgnividyā* knew the existence of the myth of Agni's descent which already belonged to the Jaiminīya tradition, or that he heard AitB 3.33 and introduced it into the JB.

and coals, we can suggest that two of them are mentioned in the relevant passage of the JB:

JB 3.263 — Those (animals) that first came into existence are the red ones; those that came into existence out of the (seed) when it was being heated, are the reddish brown ones; those that came into existence out of the (seed) when it was heated, are the brown ones; those that came into existence out of the (seed), when it was being burned, are the mules and the black (animals), and therefore, this same fire burns the white as well as the black (animal); out of the *sparks* were created the goats and the antelopes; out of the *coals* the Aṅgirases.

So I suppose that the columns and their headers were first added with the association partly from JB 3.263, and then the cells were filled with the words related to the relevant fire.

Now the question is how X and Y were filled. We know from JB 1.45 that X is "immortality, the (heavenly) waters" and that Y is "night". This point is quite important for us, because it causes the cosmological problem discussed by Schmithausen (1994: 56). The fuel of the third dimension is atmosphere. That of the second dimension is heaven. That of the first dimension is night. So night is located above heaven. The cosmos here has a quadripartite structure, instead of the normal tripartite one. My answer comes again from the myth of Agni's descent:

JB 3.262-263 — Now, Prajāpati had set his mind on his own daughter, the Dawn. She, having become a red deer, stood for him. He, having become a spotted deer, leaped on her. He saw, "For this did the gods create me, for carefully watching. This one transgresses. Well, I will pierce him." He pierced. He (Prajāpati), pierced, having thrown away this form, and went upward. This (arrow shot by Rudra) is (the constellation called) "the three-knotted arrow".

The existence of the Dawn suggests that the act is played in the morning. The point is that the night sky with stars is extended above, seemingly over heaven[257]. The inventor of the *pañcāgnividyā* must have taken the "night" from here and put it over "heaven" in the scheme of the proto-*pañcāgnividyā*. The "stars" and the "moon" were put in the columns for

[257] Remember that the original cast was Heaven instead of Prajāpati. See Chapter 3.

the sparks and coals respectively. The "day" for the flame seems to have been filled by the association from the "night", and the "ray of the sun" for the smoke by the association from the sun.

The fact that the myth of Agni's descent was used to construct the *pañcāgnividyā* must mean that its inventor was conscious of the whole myth-ritual complex around it. Thus, the *pañcāgnividyā* was intended as a renewed version of Agni's descent. This is also clear from the JB passage directly following it. Let us borrow the translation of Bodewitz (1973) again.

JB 1.46 [And when he goes to yonder world] his (funeral) fire is Agni Vaiśvānara. Its fuel is the herbs and trees, its flame is just the flame (of the fire), its smoke just the smoke, its sparks just the sparks, its coals just the coals. In this same Agni Vaiśvānara the gods day by day offer man. From this oblation when it has been offered man comes into existence (and goes) to yonder world. That is for him the world in which he resurges.[258]

The fire mentioned here is the cremation fire, which brings the deceased sacrificer to heaven. That this text follows the *pañcāgnividyā* with obvious stylistic continuity means that here the myth of Agni's descent is combined with the ascension of the deceased through the cosmic Agni. And this must be the reason why a description of the funeral rite is inserted after this text, in the middle of the elucidation of the Agnihotra. The crucial point of the JB funeral rite is the following mantra, which we can now clearly understand as an expression of the combined processes of the ascent and the descent of fire.

JB 1.47 He has come into existence through thee, thou through him. He is thy womb, his womb thou art. As a father clearing the way for his son lead him, Jātavedas, to the world of the virtuous. From him thou wast born, he must be born from thee, *svāhā*.[259]

---

[258] *[atha yathāmuṃ lokam apyeti] tasyāgnir evāgnir vaiśvānaraḥ / tasyauṣadhayaś ca vanaspatayaś ca samit / jyotir eva jyotiḥ / dhūma eva dhūmaḥ / viṣphuliṅgā eva viṣphuliṅgāḥ / aṅgārā evāṅgārāḥ / tasminn etasminn agnau vaiśvānare 'harahar devāḥ puruṣaṃ juhvati / tasyā āhuter hutāyai puruṣo 'muṃ lokaṃ saṃbhavati / so 'sya lokaḥ punar utthāyai bhavati //*

[259] *ayaṃ vai tvad asmād asi tvam / etad ayaṃ te yonir asya yonis tvam // pitā putrāya lokakṛj jātavedo nayā hy enaṃ sukṛtāṃ yatra lokaḥ // asmād vai tvam ajāyathā eṣa tvaj jāyatāṃ svāhā //*

As I already called some attention to above, the original form of the *pañcāgnividyā* was a pure water doctrine. A fire doctrine was constructed in such a way that it traced the flow of the water. Now the ring was closed and the circulation of fire was formed. But what is the difference between the circulation of water and the circulation of fire? I think that there is a definite difference, and it is the existence of the implicit motif of self. Water circulates through heaven and earth, but it is concerned with no personality. In contrast, fire is always personal and you are burned with your own fire when you are cremated[260]. As Bodewitz (1973: 249) asserts, the JB version of the *pañcāgnividyā* does not present the concept of rebirth. However, the formation of the circulation of fire is a definitive step towards it, because it strongly stimulates the association of a personality which circulates together with fire.

The JB version of the *pañcāgnividyā* combined two lines of thoughts, namely Agni's ascent in the cremation and his descent in the Third Soma-Pressing. An even important point of this event is that it happened in the context of the Agnihotra, the daily evening and morning offering, because it obviously presents a correspondence between the daily movement of the sun and the cosmic circulation of fire. It seems plausible to me that the inventor of the *pañcāgnividyā* noticed at a certain moment the significance of his new fire doctrine and used it to integrate old mythological motifs into the framework of the Agnihotra. Here I would like to draw your attention to JB 1.3-4, which states that the Agnihotra is a concentrated form of larger rituals, especially of the Soma rituals. Indeed, the Agnihotra can now be understood as an integrated ritual, which includes heaven and earth, birth and death, and the cosmic fire which flows through them incessantly. And this must be the reason why the following statement appears in the very beginning of JB.

JB 1.1	Here now they say: "What does he offer, in what there is offered?". He offers life, in (the) life(breath) there is offered.[261]

Paul Horsch (1971) collected early instances of Vedic reincarnation doctrines. His work is the starting point for everyone who talks about its

---

[260] Cf. JB 1.2 (translated by Bodewitz): "Now when the mind passes away, when the breath, sight, hearing, then it enters these fires. Thereupon they throw after (these life-breaths) also this body of his in these fires (reciting) 'From him thou wert born, he should be born out of thee, *svāhā*'." Cf. Heesterman (1995): "Das Feuer — sei es Herd- oder Opferfeuer — ist also das *alter ego* des Menschen, auf Leben und Tod mit ihm verbunden."

[261] *tad āhuḥ kena juhoti kasmin hūyata iti / prāṇenaiva juhoti prāṇe hūyate //*

development today[262]. However, Horsch did not pay any special attention to the *pañcāgnividyā*. It is Bodewitz (1996) who supplemented his discussion from this viewpoint. He argues that there are two streams in the development of the speculation about death and rebirth: one is concerned with the origin of life in connection with the exchange between heaven and earth, and this stream finally led to the formation of the *pañcāgnividyā*. The other stream is the one that led to the Two Paths Doctrine, and it is concerned with the attainment of the immortality through the journey to heaven. Bodewitz' observation is quite reasonable. At least we see very little trace of the speculation about *karman* in the former stream, while it plays a crucially important role in the latter. In other words, the formation of the *pañcāgnividyā* was not driven by the idea of *karman* and *punarmṛtyu*. Also, it was not directly connected to the stream which Horsch took as the mainstream of the reincarnation doctrine. However, this does not necessarily mean that the *pañcāgnividyā* was a historically isolated development. When it presented the image of the circulating fire, people confronted the problem "what is the invariable subject which experiences the totality of this migration?" for the first time. And when this question was asked, they already stood in front of the concept "the immortal self". As long as one understands the *pañcāgnividyā* as a pure water doctrine, one cannot see this point, because the motif of "self" does not exist in the water doctrine.

I deliberately did not mention the "interiorization of fire" in the above discussion about the formation of the *pañcāgnividyā*, although it remains a hot topic for many of the researchers. The reason for it is that we cannot attest its involvement in the formation of *pañcāgnividyā* with our primary sources. It is also doubtful whether there is a sensible difference

---

[262] According to him, its formation took place in the following steps. 1) In the early period people already noticed that there are cyclic patterns in nature, especially the movement of the heavenly bodies. 2) The concept of the eternal return existed. 3) The idea that man can be reborn as an animal or a plant existed. 4) Magical fertility rites showed the replay of the cosmogony. 5) There existed the belief of man's rebirth as an offspring of himself. 6) At a certain moment, speculations arose about the life after death and its dependence on the merit of the rituals which one carried out in his life. 7) They further thought that those who do not participate in rituals remain in the realm of mortality. 8) The concept of *punarmṛtyu* appeared, which conveys that even those who participated in rituals die again in the life after death when the merit of the ritual runs out. 9) The importance of the esoteric knowledge increased to overcome *punarmṛtyu*. 10) Those who do not have the knowledge and cannot carry out rituals effectively die again in the life after death. Younger Brāhmaṇas say that the death in this world results in the re-corporation and that they can return in the form of man through will.

between an exterior ritual and an interiorized ritual in the process of the transformation of myths. However, I do not deny the importance of this concept in the middle Vedic period. According to Heesterman (1995), the concept of "the immortal atman" was formed in the ritualistic field of thought, with the interiorization of fire as a medium. Although the interiorization does not seem to have played a role in the formation of the *pañcāgnividyā*, they are close to each other in the sense that they lead to the same conclusion. In other words, they were two independent threads of thought, which ran simultaneously and in parallel tracks.

Just as the speculation about *karman* is alien to the *pañcāgnividyā*, the question about the immortal self is alien to the arguments on *karman*. The latter formed the mainstream of the Indian reincarnation doctrine. The former enriched it with the motif of a limitless cyclic pattern of the Agnihotra, and finally became part of into the late Vedic arguments on the *ātman*.

In this chapter, we dealt with the *pañcāgnividyā*, which seems to be located on the intersection of the two myths covered in the previous chapters. The above discussion corresponds to the point indicated by the arrow in the concept scheme below.

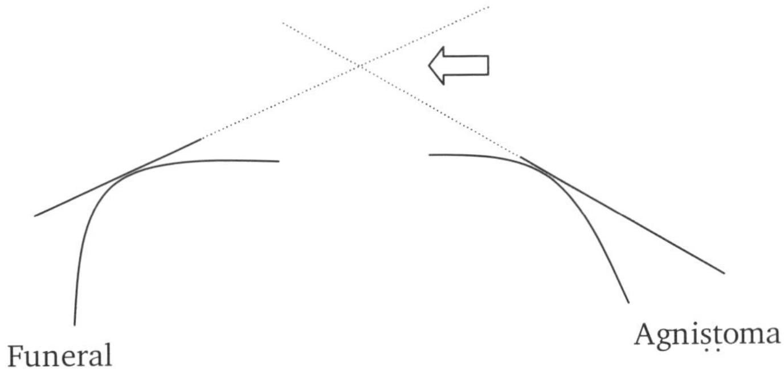

Conclusion

As we have already seen, ritual presents an isolated island in the centre of the world, in which all the worldly activities are substituted for executed rules. Within this ritual space language games do not take effect. In other words, the activities that take place do not generate any meaning. This meaninglessness of ritual procedures was our starting point, and we share it with Frits Staal. However, while Staal directly springs from here to the negation of any meaning of ritual, we further discussed some other aspects of ritual which could be understood in terms of meaning. The first of them is the meaning which is given to the ritual according to the social or personal context. When you go to a temple to pray, what your prayer means is obvious to you, while you are not always conscious of it. This meaning is disconnected from the symbolic meaning which the relevant ritual procedures might convey. To approach this type of meaning, you need in principle to observe the relevant persons and the society directly.

The second type of the meaning of ritual is what we dealt with in the above three chapters. We cannot observe the Vedic people and society directly. So we have in fact no means to know what a Vedic ritual meant to the Vedic people. However, as we discussed above, a ritual presents us with a riddle which actually has no answer. What matters in this case is not the intrinsic meaning, but the process in which the meaning is generated. So our starting point should be reconstructing the intention with which the ritual procedures were originally designed, and tracing the development of the associations from it. This approach does not aim at capturing what people experienced as the meaning of the ritual, but at capturing the historical output of the ritual practices and its meaning. In this way, we can observe how a ritual produced meaningful results.

In Chapter 1, we started from the apparent duality of Agni Vaiśvānara and reconstructed the cosmic structure of the Vedic Agni, which consists of the sun, the sacrificial fire, and the spoke which joins them. This total cosmic Agni can be called Agni Vaiśvānara, but more specifically the sun can be denoted with this name. Agni Jātavedas brings oblations through the spoke. As we have seen in the cremation mantras, the deceased sacrificer is first put in the sacrificial fire on earth, then brought upwards with Agni Jātavedas, and finally reaches the sun, namely the Agni Vaiśvānara in a narrow sense.

In Chapter 2, we reconstructed the myth of Agni's descent in RV 3.3: The sun ejaculates and the sperm falls on earth as fertile fire. The original relationship of this myth to the Svarbhānu myth which was studied by Jamison (1991) is not clear, but we can observe some traces of the interaction between these two myths. The implementation of the Third

Soma Pressing of the Agniṣṭoma ritual presupposes the myth of Agni's descent, and the motif of Prajāpati's incest, which appears in the elucidations of the relevant ritual procedure in the Brāhmaṇas, can be explained as having been imported from the context of the Svarbhānu myth.

Each of these ritual procedures has strong evocativeness. The cremation presents an image of Agni's ascent. The end of the sacrificer's life is connected to his sacrificial fire and its movement towards heaven through the structure of the cosmic Agni, from the navel of earth to the top of heaven. The Third Soma Pressing and RV 3.3 which is recited present the image of the sun's ejaculation and its sperm's descent. Sperm implies propagation. So this ritual procedure evokes the idea of the derivation of earthly lives from heaven.

In Chapter 3 we treated the *pañcāgnividyā*, which is located on the crossing point of two mysteries. We observed that a new scheme was invented in which the upward fire and the downward fire were combined with each other and formed a circulation. This new complex of fire myths joined the existing concept of the circulation of water, and formed a new concept of circulation which renewed the old Rigvedic one. In other words, a new mystery was born, which inherited the evocativeness of all the motifs of the preceding stages. — What is life? It is the circulation of fire, which contains the ascending fire, the descending fire, heaven, earth, ejaculating sun, ejaculating myself, past, future, offspring, ancestors. Life is not only the period between your birth and death, but it has multiple dimensions. And all these associations are connected back to the Agnihotra, the daily evening and morning offerings. And a new stage starts, in which the newly formed mystery asks you: How is this circulation maintained? How would you live in this limitless circulation? How does it cease?

In short, ritual was a cradle of archaic philosophy in India. Mythological concepts were synthesized in the ritual context, and its results gave a new interpretation to the rituals themselves and to the life of man. An important point here is that the process of this development contains practices. In other words, there were innumerable ritual practices before the doctrine was born from the myths. In these practices people engraved the myths in their own bodies by reciting verses and executing ritual actions. People did not only understand the motifs of upward and downward movement of fire, but also physically enacted them. And while people continued to carry them out, at a certain moment the potential structure of the rituals began to be visible to them: the cremation and the Third Soma Pressing together form a circle, and it is isomorphic to the Agnihotra. In other words, the *modus operandi* of the ritualists found its own way from myths towards philosophy.

Maurice Bloch (1986) discusses the problem of the historicity of rituals in the last chapter of his monograph on the circumcision ritual in

Madagascar. He starts from the theoretical problem of the basic viewpoints, namely functionalism and intellectualism. He wonders why they always fail to explain rituals, and indicates that both of these approaches do not take into account the fact that rituals are events that combine the properties of statements and actions. In other words, the intellectualist approach considers the ritual as a statement, and the functionalist one as an action. Both of them only look at one side of rituals. To avoid this problem he approaches the ritual by analyzing how it is manifested in history, and notices that the symbolic system of the circumcision ritual has changed very little during 200 years while the social environment and the function of the ritual in it have changed dramatically. However, if ideology were the product of circumstances, it would change when they do. Why does the symbolic system not change according to the change of the environment? He tries to answer it from the viewpoint of the theory of ideology: The circumcision ritual establishes the authority of everyone, and this emotional rightness leads to collusion between inferiors and superiors, which gives the ritual an ideological power to survive politico-economic changes. And the rulers used the ready-made symbolic system that was already there, because it was so fundamental and beyond question. Thus, according to Bloch, the stability of the ritual tells us something of the nature of ideology.

Although Bloch's work is excellent in other regards, this argument does not seem convincing. At least, it looks like a tautology, which presupposes that ritual is a kind of ideology and concludes that ritual can work as an ideology. Moreover, it is quite doubtful that we can talk about ritual in terms of ideology in principle. As we have already discussed, the symbolic system of a ritual is disconnected from the meaning of the ritual which is experienced by the participants. This means that the intention with which the symbolic system was originally designed cannot be conducted to the participants as the meaning of the ritual. In that case, how could the ideological power of a ritual be assured? As Bloch himself mentions, it can happen that a ritual's symbolic system conveys a ridiculous statement like "men have no part in procreation" while people know that it is complete nonsense. If the symbolic system would really be an ideological product, there would be a conflict here. The fact that the absurd image can exist in and around the ritual shows that people understand it as belonging to the disconnected ritual space. And if this is so, we cannot reduce ritual to ideology. Of course it is true that some rituals were artificially designed to function as propaganda, and we can pick up some examples from the time of the Second World War, especially among the countries where public opinion was manipulated in a less refined, direct way. However, it does not necessarily mean that rituals are essentially ideological, but they can possibly be exploited. The stability of rituals, as Bloch puts it, does not come from the ideological character of the ritual, but from the disconnection between the functional aspect and the symbolic system of the ritual.

Thus the symbolic system of a ritual cannot be reduced to the social function of the ritual. It can be exploited *ad hoc* for the implementation of social functions, but in principle it is an isolated story told in the disconnected space, and its original intention is not guaranteed to reach the actual life of people who carry out the ritual. The true meaning of the symbolic system consists in the various new concepts which it historically generates while invoking people's imagination.

I would like to talk about cherry blossoms, because it looks like the best way to show what the historicity of rituals means. Like any other Japanese I love to see cherry blossoms. My wife is not Japanese, and although she can of course appreciate their beauty, the cherry blossoms that she sees are not the same blossoms as I see. What I see there is not only the beautiful form and color of the blossoms, but the whole literary tradition of the archipelago presented through the image of the blooming and falling cherry blossoms — tears of Saigyō, sighs of Tsurayuki, silence of Bashō, delicacy of Tanizaki, and innumerable kinds of emotions of thousands of other writers and creators. My own aesthetic feelings have been cultivated within this tradition, and whenever I see cherry blossoms I recognize myself there. The viewing of cherry blossoms develops aesthetics, and the development of aesthetics enriches your viewing of the blossoms. Time goes by and cherry blossoms appear more and more beautiful to you, while they actually remain the same. And such a process is not at all peculiar to the Japanese. Any French person who remembers Rimbaud's poem may think of eternity when he sees the sunset in the sea. The Americans who go to a baseball game maintain a great collection of the memories of all the games they have ever seen, and it enriches the game which they are watching. Precisely in the same way, the development of the associations around the exchange of fire between heaven and earth resulted in the enriching of the concept of life. As the cherry blossoms show themselves differently for those who are in the Japanese literal tradition, the Agnihotra is experienced differently by those who know what it is, and life is experienced differently by those who carry out the Agnihotra. So I would like to conclude our discussion: Ritual is pure activity without meaning or goal, but is not meaningless in the sense that it generates meanings.

Appendix: Mātariśvan, Heaven, Underworld

Before Kuiper (1971), Mātariśvan was thought to bring Agni only from heaven. Kuiper noticed that the word *parāvátaḥ* "from afar" denotes the underworld[263], and indicated that some of the Rigvedic Mātariśvan passages describe the derivation of fire from the underworld, not from heaven. The passages that he cites can indeed most naturally be interpreted in that way, and so he does appear to be right. However, this new interpretation revealed a certain inconsistency in the Rigvedic Mātariśvan myth: there are some Rigvedic passages which explicitly say that Agni is brought by Mātariśvan from heaven.

Kuiper (1971: 94) mentions this problem, but his explanation sounds somewhat ambiguous[264]. Although his work has a great significance in that he corrected the mistake of earlier studies, this point must still be answered. Why are there two different types of statements concerning from whence Mātariśvan brought fire?

Chronological Scan

The first approach we could try might be a chronological one. Following Converse (1971) and Bodewitz (1994), I assume 5 layers in the Rigveda: I. Books 2-7, II. 1.51-191, III. Book 8 and 1.1-50, IV. Book 9, V. Book 10. We will examine the relevant material in each layer.

In Stratum I, Mātariśvan appears in 3.2.13, 3.5.9, 3.5.10, 3.9.5, 3.26.2, 3.29.11, and 6.8.4. Among these, Mātariśvan is said to bring Agni "from afar" in 3.9.5 and 6.8.4:

---

[263] See Kuiper (1960: 226) and Kuiper (1964: 107).

[264] "It remains one of the unsolved problems of Vedic mythology why terms for 'nether world' and 'primeval world' can alternate with 'heaven', 'the highest heaven', 'the third heaven'. Possibly these terms primarily denoted the mysterious world of the totality of the dualistic cosmos, Viṣṇu's third step, and were then also used in application to the undivided primeval world. Be that as it may, this much is obvious that the *parāvát*, which could be identified with *Nírṛti-*, was not a dwelling-place of the Devas." Kuiper seems to be hesitating to apply his own theory to this problem, and just says: "The same equivalence of the distant region (*parāvát-*) and heaven is found in the myth of Mātariśvan. On the one hand Mātariśvan is said to have brought Agni for Manu from afar: 1.128.2 *yám mātariśvā mánave parāváto, devám bhā́ḥ parāvátaḥ*, while on the other hand Mātariśvan brought Agni from heaven (*divó*), in constrast with Soma who is said to have come from the rock."

RV 3.9.5 Mātariśvan led Agni, who has, so to say, run away by himself, who was hidden there, who was kindled, *from afar* for the gods[265].

RV 6.8.4 In the lap of the waters, the buffaloes seized [him]. The kinsmen have worshipped the praiseworthy king. The messenger of Vivasvat brought Agni. Mātariśvan [brought] Vaiśvānara *from afar*[266].

3.2.13 gives us different information:

RV 3.2.13 Mātariśvan took the regular, sacrifice-worthy, inspired, praiseworthy one, *who dwelt in heaven*. We beg Agni, who has conspicuous way, who has golden hair, who shines well, for a new good advance[267].

"Who dwelt in heaven" (*diví kṣáyam*)[268] implies the derivation of Agni from heaven.

3.5.9 and 10 do not mention the place from whence Agni is brought: RV 3.5.9 "Being praised, the youngest one has glared up with the fire-wood towards the hight of heaven at the navel of earth. When Agni is invoked as Mitra, Mātariśvan, the messenger, carries the gods for the offering[269]." RV 3.5.10 "Agni, [flaming] high with the fire-wood, being the highest of the lights, has propped up the firmament, when Mātariśvan has kindled him, who was hidden for the the Bhṛgus as an oblation-carrier[270]."

3.26.2 and 3.29.11 do not seem to be concerned with the bringing of Agni: RV 3.26.2 "We call him, the bright Agni, for help. [We call] Vaiśvānara, Mātariśvan, who is praiseworthy. [We call] Bṛhaspati for the divine service of human. [We call] the inspired hearer, the guest who

---

[265] *sasṛvā́ṃsam iva tmánāgním itthā́ tiróhitam / aínaṃ nayan mātaríśvā parāváto devébhyo mathitám pári.*

[266] *apā́m upásthe mahiṣā́ agṛbhṇata víśo rā́jānam úpa tasthur ṛgmíyam / ā́ dūtó agním abharad vivásvato vaiśvānarám mātaríśvā parāvátaḥ //*

[267] *ṛtā́vānaṃ yajníyaṃ vípram ukthyàm ā́ yáṃ dadhé mātaríśvā diví kṣáyam / táṃ citráyāmaṃ hárikeśam īmahe sudītím agníṃ suvitā́ya návyase //*

[268] Geldner notes: "*diví kṣáyam* ist unfertiges Bahuvrīhikompositum, vgl. 10.63.5, 8.64.4 und 8.15.9", and he translates it "da er in Himmel wohnte".

[269] *úd u ṣṭutáḥ samídhā yahvó adyaud várṣman divó ádhi nā́bhā pṛthivyā́ḥ / mitró agnír ī́ḍyo mātaríśvā dūtó vakṣad yajáthāya devā́n //*

[270] *úd astambhīt samídhā nā́kam ṛṣvò 'gnír bhávann uttamó rocanā́nām / yádī bhṛ́gubhyaḥ pári mātaríśvā gúhā sántaṃ havyavā́haṃ samīdhé //*

runs rapidly[271]." RV 3.29.11 "The asuric embryo is called Tanūnapāt. When he is born, he becomes Narāśaṃsa. [He is] Mātariśvan, when he is formed in [his] mother. He became the gust of wind at [his] advance[272]."

Stratum II. The following verses explicitly state that Mātariśvan brings Agni from heaven.

RV 1.93.6 Mātariśvan brought one (Agni) *from heaven*, the eagle stole the other from the rock. O Agni and Soma, being strengthened by the prayer, you have made a wide world for the sacrifice[273].

RV1.143.2 *Being born in the highest heaven, Agni became manifest for Mātariśvan*. When he was kindled by the magical power and greatness, his flame illuminated Heaven and Earth[274].

In the following verse, Agni is brought "from afar":

RV 1.128.2 We make the accomplisher of sacrifice intimate with us by the way of the Ṛta with the salutation accompanied with offering, with the divine service accompanied with offering. By the offering of our tonic, he does not become old in the appearance. [We make intimate with us] the god whom Mātariśvan brought *from afar* to Manu, *from afar*[275].

The following verse mentions "the shaker of mead" (*mádhva ādhavé*):

RV 1.141.3 When the ruling lords liberate him from the depth, from the form of a buffalo with power, when

---

[271] *táṃ śubhrám agním ávase havāmahe vaiśvānarám mātaríśvānam ukthyàm / bṛ́haspátim mánuṣo devátātaye vípraṃ śrótāram átitiṃ raghuṣyádam //*

[272] *tánūnápād ucyate gárbha āsuró nárāśáṃso bhavati yád vijā́yate / mātaríśvā yád ámimīta mātári vā́tasya sárgo abhavat sárīmaṇi //*

[273] *ā́nyám divó mātaríśvā jabhārā́mathnād anyám pári śyenó ádreḥ / ágnīṣomā bráhmaṇā vāvṛdhānórúṃ yajñā́ya cakrathur u lokám //*

[274] *sá jā́yamānaḥ paramé vyòmany āvír agnír abhavan mātaríśvane / asyá krátvā samidhānásya majmánā prá dyā́vā śocíḥ pṛthivī́ arocayat //*

[275] *táṃ yajñasā́dham ápi vātayāmasy ṛtásya pathā́ námasā havíṣmatā devátātā havíṣmatā / sá na ūrjā́m upā́bhṛty ayā́ kṛpā́ ná jūryati / yám mātaríśvā mánave parāváto devám bhā́ḥ parāvátaḥ //*

Mātariśvan steals him, who was hidden in *the shaker of mead* since a long time[276].

If "the shaker of mead" denotes the underworld where the subterranean water is, Agni is here also brought from the underworld.

The other verses do not mention the place Agni is brought from: 1.60.1 "Mātariśvan brought for Bhṛgu Agni, who is the famous carrier, the banner of distribution, the mindful messenger, who reaches object immediately, who has twofold birth, who is praised like wealth, as a present[277]", 1.96.4 "Mātariśvan, who has wealthy welfare, the procurer of the heavenly light, found the way for the offspring. He is the herdsman of the settlements, the begetter of both worlds. The gods hold Agni, the treasure-impeller[278]", 1.148.1 "When Mātariśvan churned out the Hotṛ, who has every form, who belongs to all the gods, whom they put down in the human settlements like the sun, who shines forth brightly for wonder[279]", 1.164.46 "They call [him] Indra, Mitra, Varuṇa [and] Agni. And he is the heavenly bird Garutmat. The inspired ones speak variously about it, which is unique. They call [it] Agni, Yama, [and] Mātariśvan[280]", 1.190.2 "The speeches regularly strive for him, who is discharged like a discharging of those who worship gods, because Bṛhaspati, who quickly extends over the wide spaces, became Mātariśvan at the Ṛta[281]", RV 1.71.4 "When Mātariśvan, [as the fire was] distributed, churned it, and he became white and noble in every house, then Bhṛgavāna followed his duty as a messenger, just like being in attendance on a more powerful king[282]."

Stratum III contains two verses:

RV 1.31.3 O Agni, be first manifest for Mātariśvan with the good magical power for Vivasvat. Heaven and Earth trembled

[276] *nír yád īm bhdhnā́n mahiṣásya várpasa ī́śānā́saḥ śávasā kránta sūráyaḥ / yád īm ánu pradívo mádhva ādhavé gúhā sántam mātaríśvā mathāyáti //*

[277] *váhniṃ yaśásaṃ vidáthasya ketúṃ suprāvyàṃ dūtáṃ sadyóartham / dvijánmānaṃ rayím iva praśastáṃ rātím bharad bhṛ́gave mātaríśvā //*

[278] *sá mātaríśvā puruvā́rapuṣṭir vidád gātúṃ tánayāya svarvít / viśā́ṃ gopā́ janitā́ ródasyor devā́ agníṃ dhārayan draviṇodā́m //*

[279] *máthīd yád īṃ viṣṭó mātaríśvā hótāraṃ viśvā́psum viśvádevyam / ní yáṃ dadhúr manuṣyā̀su vikṣú svàr ṇá citráṃ vápuṣe vibhā́vam //*

[280] *índram mitráṃ váruṇam agním āhur átho divyáḥ sá suparṇó garútmān / ékaṃ sád víprā bahudhā́ vadanty agníṃ yamám mātaríśvānam āhuḥ //*

[281] *tám ṛtvíyā úpa vā́caḥ sacante sárgo ná yó devayatā́m ásarji / bṛ́haspátiḥ sá hy áñjo várāṃsi víbhvā́bhavat sám ṛté mātaríśvā //*

[282] *máthīd yád īṃ víbhṛto mātaríśvā gṛhé-gṛhe śyetó jényo bhū́t / ā́d īṃ rā́jñe ná sáhīyase sácā sánn ā́ dūtyàm bhṛ́gavāṇo vivāya //*

at the Hotṛ-selection. You became a match for the burden. You sacrificed to the great, o Vasu[283].

1.31.3 is parallel to 1.143.2 "Being born in the highest heaven, Agni became manifest for Mātariśvan". This can also be regarded as the derivation of Agni from heaven. 8.52.2 does not indicate the place: "O Indra, [just as] you were intoxicated with the pressed [Soma] at Pṛṣadra, Medhya, [and] Mātariśvan, just as [you drank] Soma at Daśaśipra, Daśoṇya, Syūmaraśmi [and] Ṛjūnas[284]".

Stratum IV contains one verse: 9.67.31 "The one who learns the Pavamāna-verses by heart eats the essence which was brought together by the Ṛṣis, the all which is purified, which was made sweet by Mātariśvan[285]". This also does not specify the place.

Stratum V. RV 10.46.9 "[They have put] Agni, whom heaven and earth begot, whom the waters, Tvaṣṭṛ, [and] the Bhṛgus [begot] with power. Mātariśvan [and] the gods have formed the sacrifice-worthy one, who is to be invoked first, for Manu[286]." 10.105.6: "He praised by the lofty power with the lofty ones. The brave one, Mātariśvan, has formed [the club] with power just as Ṛbhu [forms it] with the magical power[287]". 10.85.47: "Let all the gods and waters melt the heart of us two together. Let Mātariśvan, the creator and directress, put us together[288]". 10.48.2: "I am Indra, the wall [and] breast-[plate] of the Atharvans. For Trita, I released cows from the Dragon. I took manly power from the Dasyus, teaching the cowherds to go to Dadhyañc [and] Mātariśvan[289]". 10.88.19: "Before the winged one wears the face of Uṣas, o Mātariśvan, the Brahmin puts [him], going to the sacrifice, sitting down against the Hotṛ[290]". 10.109.1 "They, [namely] the limitless ocean, Mātariśvan, the heat which

---

283 *tvám agne prathamó mātaríśvana āvír bhava sukratūyā́ vivásvate / árejetāṃ ródasī hotṛvū́ryé 'saghnor bhārám áyajo mahó vaso //*

284 *pṛ́ṣadhre médhye mātaríśvanī́ndra suvāné ámandathāḥ / yáthā sómaṃ dáśaśipre dáśoṇye syū́maraśmāv ṛ́jūnasi //*

285 *yáḥ pāvamānī́r adhyéty ṛ́ṣibhiḥ sámbhṛtaṃ rásam / sárvaṃ sá pūtám aśnāti svaditám mātariśvanā.*

286 *dyā́vā yám agním pṛthivī́ jániṣṭām ā́pas tváṣṭā bhṛ́gavo yáṃ sáhobhiḥ / īḷényam prathamám mātaríśvā devā́s tatakṣur mánave yájatram //*

287 *prā́staud ṛṣvaújā ṛṣvébhis tatákṣa śū́raḥ śávasā / ṛbhúr ná krátubhir mātaríśvā //*

288 *sam añjantu víśve devā́ḥ sám ā́po hṛ́dayāni nau / sám mātaríśvā sáṃ dhātā́ sám u déṣṭrī dadhātu nau //*

289 *ahám índro ródho vákṣo átharvaṇas tritā́ya gā́ ajanayam áher ádhi / ahám dásyubhyaḥ pári nṛmṇám ā́ dade gotrā́ śíkṣan dadhīcé mātaríśvane //*

290 *yāvanmātrám uṣáso ná prátīkaṃ suparṇyò vásate mātariśvaḥ / tā́vad dadhāty úpa yajñám āyán brāhmaṇó hótur ávaro niṣī́dan //*

has strong flame, the terrible, benevolent one, the goddesses waters, the one who was first born with the Ṛta, spoke first about the offence against a Brahmin[291]", and 10.114.1 "The two heats, which are next to each other, have filled the threefold [world]. Mātariśvan has enjoyed them. They, desiring to obtain the heavenly milk, flew. The gods know the song of priase which is accompanied by a melody[292]".

In the later Saṃhitās, Mātariśvan is not often mentioned as the carrier of Agni. MS 4.14.15 is the same verse as RV 1.148.1, which we have already seen. RV 1.93.6, in which Mātariśvan is said to bring Agni from heaven, appears also in MS 4.14.18, TS 4.1.4.1 and KS 4.16.

As the above material shows, both of the motifs "Mātariśvan brings Agni from the underworld" and "Mātariśvan brings Agni from heaven" appear in Stratum I and II. In Stratum III, we see one instance of the motif "Mātariśvan brings Agni from heaven". We cannot distinguish these motifs in Strata IV and V. These facts mean: (1) We cannot chronologically differentiate between these two motifs. As far as our existing material is concerned, we cannot say that one motif is a later development of the other. (2) Current discussion on the Vedic concept of "life after death" makes it clear that the other alternations indicated by Kuiper are observed in the latest layers of the Rigveda[293]. In contrast, the alternation of the place from whence Mātariśvan brings Agni can be observed in the first three layers. Therefore Mātariśvan should be treated separately from the alternation of the Pitṛs, Yama, and Varuṇa. (3) These motifs become much less important in the newer strata.

Conceptual Scheme

Let us approach our motifs from a different angle. In which context are these motifs related?

It is conspicuous that the motif "Mātariśvan brings Agni from heaven" is related in the context of Agni's birth in heaven and the establishment of Agni as the sacrificial fire on earth:

RV 1.143.1	I present a powerful new hymn, a hymn of the speech to Agni, the son of strength, the dear son of water who sat down with the Vasus on earth as a pleasant Hotṛ, the regular one[294].

---

[291] *tè 'vadan prathamā́ brahmakilbiṣé 'kūpāraḥ saliló mātaríśvā / vīḷúharās tápa ugró mayobhū́r ā́po devī́ḥ prathamajā́ ṛténa //*

[292] *gharmā́ sámantā trivṛ́taṃ vy ā̀patus táyor júṣṭim mātaríśvā jagāma / divás páyo dídhiṣāṇā aveṣan vidúr devā́ḥ sahásāmānam arkám //*

[293] See Bodewitz (1994) and Butzenberger (1996).

[294] *prá távyasīṃ návyasīṃ dhītím agnáye vācó matíṃ sáhasaḥ sūnáve bhare / apā́ṃ nápād yó vásubhiḥ sahá priyó hótā pṛthivyā́ṃ ny ásīdad ṛtvíyaḥ //*

RV 1.143.2 *Being born in the highest heaven, Agni became manifest for Mātariśvan*. When he was kindled by the magical power and greatness, his flame illuminated Heaven and Earth

RV 1.143.3 The glaring, ageless rays of Agni, who has beautiful appearance, who has a beautiful face, who shines beautifully, who has the power of the light, trembles without sleeping, without aging, just like rivers at night[295] [296].

RV 1.143.4 Send forth with songs in [your] own house Agni, the all-knowing, *whom Bhṛgus have put down on the navel of the earth*, with the power of the world, who, as a unique one, rules over wealth like Varuṇa[297].

1.143.2 and 4ab refer to the events in the past. In these verses, Agni's birth, Mātariśvan's deed, and the Bhṛgu's establishment of the sacrificial fire can be interpreted as sequential events. RV 3.2 gives another instance:

RV 3.2.10 The human tonics made the seer of the settlements, the chief of the settlements, sharp like an axe. He goes upwards and downwards, while working. He puts the embryo in these beings[298].

RV 3.2.11 The procreating seed bull incites himself into the conspicuous wombs, while roaring like a lion. Vaiśvānara,

---

295 *áty aktúr*: Oldenberg and Geldner take it as adnominal. This seems more natural than the interpretation by Grassmann, who takes it as adverbial (see his Wörterbuch under *áti*). But *aktúr* is the nominative form. Oldenberg conjectures *áty aktū́ṁr* > *áty aktúr*. Geldner thinks that it is a haplology of *áty aktúm aktúr* "die Nacht über gleich dem Farbenspiel". Renou notes: "peut-être un ancien *aktū́n ná síndhavaḥ* a-t-il été remplacé par *aktúḥ* sous l'influence du type *sindhur ná kṣódaḥ*" (EVP 12 p.105), and translates "par delà (les nuits) comme la surface-ointe". There are no decisive grounds to adopt any one of these.

296 *asyá tveṣā́ ajárā asyá bhānávaḥ susaṃdṛ́śaḥ suprátīkasya sudyútaḥ / bhā́tvakṣaso áty aktúr ná síndhavo 'gné rejante ásasanto ajárāḥ //*

297 *yám eriré bhṛ́gavo viśvávedasaṃ nā́bhā pṛthivyā́ bhúvanasya majmánā / agníṃ táṃ gīrbhír hinuhi svá ā́ dáme yá éko vásvo váruṇo ná rā́jati //*

298 *viśā́ṃ kavíṃ viśpátim mā́nuṣīr íṣaḥ sáṃ sīm akṛṇvan svádhitiṃ ná téjase / sá udváto niváto yāti véviṣat sá gárbham eṣú bhúvaneṣu dīdharat //*

	who has a wide surface, the immortal one, who distributes the treasure and wealth for a pious one[299].
RV 3.2.12	Vaiśvānara has ascended heaven as in the ancient time. Being honoured by good singers, he [ascends] the top of heaven. Producing the wealth for people as before, the watchful one goes round the same course[300].
RV 3.2.13	*Mātariśvan put the regular, sacrifice-worthy, inspired, praiseworthy one, who dwelt in heaven.* We go to Agni, who has a conspicuous way, who has golden hair, who shines well, for a new good advance.

This passage was discussed above as an instance of "Agni's birth in heaven" = Heaven's ejaculation. In 3.2.10-12, Agni Vaiśvānara releases the sperm. The sperm is infused into "these beings" (3.2.11) or "the conspicuous wombs" (3.2.11), which seems to be the plant from which the churning sticks are taken[301]. 3.2.13ab can be interpreted as the establishment of the sacrificial fire.

As was also discussed above, RV 1.31 contrasts Agni's birth on earth with Agni's birth in heaven:

RV 1.31.3	O Agni, be first manifest for Mātariśvan with the good magical power for Vivasvat. *Heaven and Earth* trembled at the Hotṛ-selection. You became a match for the burden. You sacrificed to the great, o Vasu.
RV 1.31.4	O Agni, you caused Heaven to roar for a man. For the benevolent Purūravas, a more benevolent one [caused Heaven to roar]. When you are released at the *parents* with the power, they lead you around forward and again backward[302].

In 1.31.4, Agni is born from the parents = the churning sticks, through the movement "forward and again backward". As already mentioned above, 3ab is parallel to 1.143.2, which explicitly relates Agni's birth in heaven. "Heaven and Earth" in 1.31.3 corresponds to the "parents" in

---

299 *sá jinvate jaṭháreṣu prajajñivā́n vŕ̥ṣā citréṣu nā́nadan ná siṃháḥ / vaiśvānaráḥ pr̥thupā́jā ámartyo vásu rátnā dáyamāno ví dāśúṣe //*

300 *vaiśvānaráḥ pratnáthā nā́kam ā́ruhad divás pr̥ṣṭhám bhándamānaḥ sumánmabhiḥ / sá pūrvaváj janáyañ jantáve dhánaṃ samānám ájmam páry eti jā́gr̥viḥ //*

301 See the section "Agni's Birth in the Highest Heaven".

302 *tvám agne mánave dyā́m avāśayaḥ purūrávase sukŕ̥te sukŕ̥ttaraḥ / śvātréṇa yát pitrór múcyase páry ā́ tvā pū́rvam anayann ā́paraṃ púnaḥ //*

1.31.4, and implies the churning out of Agni through the union of Heaven and Earth[303].

The above Rigvedic passages associate Agni's birth in heaven with the establishment of the sacrificial fire. Mātariśvan appears as a figure who combines these two elements.

As to the other motif, RV 3.9 gives a comprehensive picture of it:

RV 3.9.4	After he has escaped the faults and many droughts, the attentive, undeceivable ones have found him, *who abided in the waters* just like a lion[304].
RV 3.9.5	*Mātariśvan led Agni, who has, so to say, run away by himself, who was hidden there, who was kindled, from afar for the gods.*
RV 3.9.6	The mortals seized you, o oblation-carrier for the gods, so that you watch all the sacrifices, o humanly one, with your magical power, o the youngest one[305].
RV 3.9.9	The three thousand and three hundred thirty nine gods honoured Agni. They sprinkled Ghṛta and scattered Barhis for him. And then they put him down as the Hotṛ[306].

Agni is found abiding "in the waters" in 3.9.4, and Mātariśvan brings him "from afar" = the underworld. Obviously, these two places are identical. Agni is received by people in 3.9.6, and his presence at the sacrifices is mentioned. And 3.9.9 states that Agni is put down as the Hotṛ. As far as this hymn is concerned, Agni's stay in the waters, Mātariśvan's bringing of Agni, and the establishment of the sacrificial fire are three successive events, and Mātariśvan's deed can be interpreted as combining "Agni's birth in the waters" and "establishment of the sacrificial fire on earth".

RV 1.128 gives another instance of this motif:

RV 1.128.1	This one is born in the fire-holder of Manu. The Hotṛ who sacrifices the best [is born] according to the obedience of Uśijes. Agni [is born] according to [his] own obedience. [He is] the one who listens to everything for the one who attends as a friend. [He is] like treasure

---

303 See the section "Agni's Birth in the Highest Heaven".

304 *īyivā́ṃsam áti srídhaḥ śáśvatīr áti saścátaḥ / ánv īm avindan nicirā́so adrúho apsú siṃhám iva śritám //*

305 *táṃ tvā mártā agṛbhṇata devébhyo havyavāhana / víśvān yád yajñā́m̐ abhipā́si mānuṣa táva krátvā yaviṣṭhya //*

306 *trī́ṇi śatā́ trī́ sahásrāṇy agníṃ triṃśác ca devā́ náva cāsaparyan / aúkṣan ghṛtaír ástṛṇan barhír asmā ā́d íd dhótāraṃ ny àsādayanta //*

	for the one who seeks for fame. *The undeceivable Hotṛ sits down at the place of libation, being covered at the place of libation*[307].
RV 1.128.2	We make the accomplisher of sacrifice intimate with us by the way of the Ṛta with the salutation accompanied with offering, with the divine service accompanied with offering. By the offering of our tonic, he does not become old in the appearance. [We make intimate with us] the god whom Mātariśvan brought from afar to Manu, from afar.
RV 1.128.3	He surrounds the earth with the speedy [movement] at once. Raising voice suddenly, *the seed bull [puts] sperm while roaring*, putting sperm while roaring. Seeing with hundred eyes, the god is victorious in the woods. *Putting the seat in the lower summits*, Agni, in the higher summits[308].
RV 1.128.4	Agni, the Purohita who has good magical power, gives consideration to the sacrifice and Soma sacrifice at every house. He gives consideration to the sacrifice with the magical power. With magical power, Vedhas for the one who shoots arrows has seen all the creatures, *as soon as the guest, being beautiful with Ghṛta, was born, [namely when] the draught animal, Vedhas, was born*[309].

1.128.1 "The undeceivable Hotṛ sits down at the place of libation, being covered at the place of libation" implies the establishment of the sacrificial fire. Agni's birth, which is mentioned in the same verse, can be interpreted as its birth on earth. 1.128.2 "the god whom Mātariśvan brings from a distance to Manu" mentions the derivation of Agni from the underworld. 1.128.3 "the seed bull [puts] sperm while roaring" and "Putting the seat in the higher summits" seem to imply Heaven's ejaculation = Agni's birth in heaven[310]. 1.128.4 "when the guest, being beautiful with Ghṛta, was born" is again concerned with Agni's birth on earth. As is al-

---

[307] *ayáṃ jāyata mánuṣo dhárīmaṇi hótā yájiṣṭha uśíjām ánu vratám agníḥ svám ánu vratám / viśváśruṣṭiḥ sakhīyaté rayír iva śravasyaté / ádabdho hótā ní ṣadad iḷás padé párivīta iḷás padé //*

[308] *évena sadyáḥ páry eti pā́rthivam muhurgī́ réto vṛṣabháḥ kánikradad dádhad rétaḥ kánikradat / śatáṃ cákṣāṇo akṣábhir devó váneṣu turváṇiḥ / sádo dádhāna úpareṣu sā́nuṣv agníḥ páreṣu sā́nuṣu //*

[309] *sá sukrátuḥ puróhito dáme-dame 'gnír yajñásyādhvarásya cetati krátvā yajñásya cetati / krátvā vedhā́ iṣūyaté víśvā jātā́ni paspaśe / yáto ghṛtaśrī́r átithir ájāyata váhnir vedhā́ ájāyata //*

[310] See "Agni's Birth in the Highest Heaven".

ready clear, Agni's threefold birth is related in this passage. The following passage also mentions two of Agni's births:

RV 6.8.1	Now, I praise the strength and wisdom of Jātavedas, [namely] the strong, reddish bull. For Vaiśvānara the new hymn purifies himself, just like the pure soma which is dear to Agni[311].
RV 6.8.2	*Being born in the highest heaven*, Agni, the lord of obedience, protected the obedience. Vaiśvānara, who has good magical power, measured out the Antarikṣa, and touched the vault with greatness[312].
RV 6.8.3	As the wonderful Mitra, he supported the two worlds apart. He made the darkness in between split with light. He rolled up both Dhiṣaṇās just like hides. Vaiśvānara obtained the whole strength[313].
RV 6.8.4	*In the lap of the waters*, the buffaloes seized [him]. The kinsmen have worshipped the praiseworthy king. The messenger of Vivasvat brought Agni. *Mātariśvan [brought] Vaiśvānara from afar.*

"The highest heaven" (6.8.2) and "the lap of the waters" (6.8.4) denote Agni's birth in heaven and in the waters, respectively.

The above instances of the motifs "Mātariśvan brings Agni from heaven/underworld" show that these motifs are directly connected with "Agni's birth in heaven/in the waters". And, as some of the above passages show, these motifs are connected with the establishment of the sacrificial fire. This means that the motifs of Mātariśvan had the function of integrating the threefold birth of Agni into the sacrificial fire. Through the stories of Mātariśvan, the sacrificial fire is identified with the Agnis born in heaven and in the waters.

If we understand the meaning of the motifs "Mātariśvan brings Agni from heaven/the waters" as above, we can explain the reason why there are two different motifs concerning Mātariśvan: inasmuch as there are three births for Agni, the sacrificial fire must be associated with all the three births to guarantee the completeness and consistency of Agni. Agni's birth on earth is implicitly associated with the sacrificial fire. The other two births must also be associated with it in some way. The motifs

---

311 *pṛkṣásya vṛ́ṣṇo aruṣásya nū́ sáhaḥ prá nú vocaṃ vidáthā jātávedasaḥ / vaiśvānarā́ya matír návyasī śúciḥ sóma iva pavate cā́rur agnáye //*

312 *sá jā́yamānaḥ paramé vyòmani vratā́ny agnír vratapā́ arakṣata / vy àntárikṣam amimīta sukrátur vaiśvānaró mahinā́ nā́kam aspṛśat //*

313 *vy àstabhnād ródasī mitró ádbhuto 'ntarvā́vad akṛṇoj jyótiṣā támaḥ / ví cármaṇīva dhiṣáṇe avartayad vaiśvānaró víśvam adhatta vṛ́ṣṇyam //*

of Mātariśvan must have been created from this need. If we think of it like this, the "alternation" of the place from whence Mātariśvan brings Agni is not a peculiar phenomenon at all, but it is a logical consequence of the concept "Agni's threefold birth".

Although Mātariśvan becomes less important in the later Rigvedic period, the conceptual scheme of "Agni's completeness" remained in the thoughts of Vedic ritualists, and was implemented in the classical Agnyādheya ritual[314]. See Krick (1982: 118-188) for the image of the primordial water which is associated with almost each Sambhāra-item, and especially MS 3.2.3 (Krick 1982: 119): "Die Wasser sind der Mutterschoß (*yoniḥ*) des Feuers; somit wird das Feuer auf seiner eigenen Geburtsstätte geschichtet." See also the motif "Agni's sperm" which appears in connection with Araṇī (Krick 1982: 188-203) and the story of Purūravas and Urvaśī (Krick 1982: 203-223), and especially MS 1.6.12 (Krick 1982: 205), which identifies Agni's sperm with Aśvattha Āroha, which are used as the churning sticks. She further says: "Die himmlische Abstammung des Feuers wird durch das Material der Reibhölzer (Araṇī) sowie die Gesänge, die die Feuerreibung begleiten, garantiert; die Vollkommenheit des Feuerleibes (der 'Gesamtperson Agni') wird dadurch erreicht, daß die einzelnen Teilkörper Agnis bzw. seine ihm eigenen Wohnstätten gesammelt und im Altar vereint werden[315]". She could have answered Kuiper's question from the viewpoint of the classical ritual. The sacrificial fire in the classical Agnyādheya is established with the material associated with the water, in which Agni was hidden. The fire is churned out with the churning sticks of Aśvattha, which is identified with Agni's sperm. Therefore, the sacrificial fire on earth is the unification of the fires born on earth, in the waters, and in heaven. All of them are necessary for the completeness and consistency of the sacrificial fire.

[314] The reason why these motifs became less important is unknown. Possibly the formation of the standard Agnyādheya procedure (i.e. the Sambhāra and the churning out) might have something to do with it. Once the standard procedure was formed, they did not have to create new Mātariśvan hymns, because now the completeness and the consistency of the fire was guaranteed by the ritual procedure.

[315] Krick (1982) p.99.

Bibliography

List of publications which are referred to in this work.

Text

AitB	Aitareya Brāhmaṇa
AV	Atharvaveda Saṃhitā
BĀU	Bṛhadāranyaka Upaniṣad
BaudhŚS	Baudhāyana Śrautasūtra
BD	Bṛhaddevatā
BPS	Baudhāyana Pitṛmedhasūtra
ChU	Chāndogya Upaniṣad
KS	Kāṭhaka Saṃhitā
MS	Maitrāyaṇīya Saṃhitā
Nir.	Nirukta
RV	Rigveda Saṃhitā
ŚB	Śatapatha Brāhmaṇa
TĀ	Taittirīya Āraṇyaka
TB	Taittirīya Brāhmaṇa
TS	Taittirīya Saṃhitā

Translations and commentaries

Geldner
Übersetzung: *Der Rig-veda*, Cambridge/Mass. 1951-1957.

Keith
The Veda of the Black Yajus School, Cambridge/Mass. 1914.
Rigveda Brahmanas, 1920.

Macdonell
Bṛhaddevatā, Cambridge/Mass. 1904.

Oldenberg
Noten: *Ṛgveda, Textkritische und exegetische Noten I-II*, Berlin 1909-1912.
SBE:*Vedic hymns part 2*, Sacred Books of East vol. 46, Oxford 1897.

Renou
EVP: *Études védiques et pāṇinéennes I-XVI*, Paris 1954-1967.

Tokunaga

The Bṛhaddevatā, Kyoto 1997.

Witzel and Gotō
Rig-Veda, Frankfurt am Main and Leipzig. 2007.

Reference Works

AiG: Wackernagel & Debrunner, *Altindische Grammatik,* Göttingen 1896-1957.

Grassmann: H. Grassmann, *Wörterbuch zum Rig-veda, 3., unveränderte Auflage,* Wiesbaden 1955.

Mayrhofer: M. Mayrhofer, *Etymologisches Wörterbuch des Altindoarischen,* Heidelberg 1986 - .

PW: O. Böhtlingk & R. Roth, *Sanskrit Wörterbuch,* St. Petersbutg 1855-1875.

Secondary literature

Austin, J.
1962: *How to Do Things with Words,* Oxford

Ayer, A.J.
1985: *Wittgenstein,* London

Baudrillard, J.
1994: *Simulacra and Simulation,* Ann Arbor

Bell, C.
1997: *Ritual: Perspectives and Demensions,* New York

Bloch, M.
1974: "Symbols, Song, Dance and Features of Articulation" *Archives Européenes de Sociology,* 15, 55-81
1986: *From Blessing to Violence,* Cambridge

Bodewitz, H.W.
1973: *Jaiminīya Brāhmaṇa 1, 1-65,* Leiden

1976: *The Daily Evening and Morning Offering (Agnihotra) According to the Brāhmaṇas*, Leiden
1982: "The 'marriage' of heaven and earth (JB1.145-146; PB 7.101-9; AB 4.27.5-10)", *Wiener Zeitschrift für die Kunde Südasiens 26*, 23-36
1987: "The black spor in the moon, salt, seed and the devayajana", *Kaviraj Commemoration Volume 4*, Benares, 307-313
1991: "Vedic conceptions of the Soul", *Light, Soul and Visions in the Veda*, Poona.
1994: "Life after Death in the Ṛgvedasaṃhitā", *Wiener Zeitschrift für die Kunde Südasiens 38*, 23-41.
1996: "The Pañcāgnividyā and the Pitṛyāna/Devayāna", *Studies on Indology (Professor Mukunda Madhava Sharma Felicitation Volume)*, Delhi

Boyer, P.
2002: *Religion Explained*, London

Butzenberger, K.
1996: "Ancient Indian Conceptions on Man's Destiny After Death", *Berliner Indologische Studien 9*, 55-118

Caland, W.
1896: *Die Altindischen Todten- und Bestattungsgebräuche*, Amsterdam.

Caland, W & Henry, V.
1906: *L'Agniṣṭoma*, Paris

Converse, H.S.
1971: *The Historical Significance of the First Occurences of the Doctrine of Transmigration in the Early Upaniṣads*, Columbia University.

Dulaney, S. & Fiske, A.P.
1994: Cultural Rituals and Obsessive-compulsive disorder" *Ethos*, 22 (3), 243-283

Eibl-Eibesfeldt, I.
1966: "The Fighting of Marine Iguanas" in: Huxley, ed. 475-476

Einoo, Sh.
1985: 「ブラーフマナ文献の祭式解釈」『国立民族学博物館研究報告』10巻4号

Eliade, M.

1976: "Spirit Light and Seed", *Occultism, Witchcraft, and Cultural Fashions*, Chicago, 93-119.

Findly, E.
1981: "Jātavedas in the Ṛgveda: The God of Generations", *Zeitschrift der Deutschen Morgenländischen Gesellschaft 131*.
1982: "The Meaning of Vedic Vaiśvānara", *Wiener Zeitschrift für die Kunde Südasiens 26*.

Geertz, C.
1973: *The Interpretation of Cultures*, New York

Gonda, J.
1959: *Epithets in the Ṛgveda*, The Hague.
1967: *The meaning of the sanskrit term dhāman*, Amsterdam.
1989: *Prayer and Blessing*, Leiden.

Gotō, T.
1987: *Die "I. Präsensklasse" im Vedischen*, Wien.

Hayakawa, A.
2000: "Three Steps to Heaven", *Asiatische Studien* LIV 1
2001: "Descent of Fire", *Asiatische Studien* LV 2
2003: "Mātariśvan, Heaven, Underworld", *Asiatische Studien* LVII 1

Heesterman, J.C.
1964: "Brahmin, Ritual, and Renouncer", *Wiener Zeitschrift für die Kunde Süd- und Ostasiens 8*. Also contained in Heesterman (1985).
1985: *The Inner Conflict of Tradition*, Chicago
1993: *The Broken World of Sacrifice*, Chicago
1995: "Feuer, Seele und Unserblichkeit" *Tod gewinnt der Mensch sein Selbst*, ed. Gerhard Oberhammer, Wien.

Hillebrandt, A.
1927-1929: *Vedische Mythologie I-II*, Zweite Auflage, Breslau.

Horsch, P.
1971: "Vorstufen der Indischen Seelenwanderungslehre", *Asiatische Studien 25*.

Huxley, J.

1966: “A Discussion on Ritualization of Behaviour in Animals and Man” *Philosophical Trasactions of the Royal Society of London*, Series B, No.772, 251: 247-526

Jamison, S.W.
1991: *The ravenous hyenas and the wounded sun*, Ithaca and London

Jamison, S.W.
1996: *Sacrificed Wife/Sacrificer's Wife*, New York

Kikai, A.
2003:『ウィトゲンシュタインはこう考えた』, Tokyo

Klein, J.S.
1985: *Toward a Discourse Grammar of the Rigveda Vol.1 part 1*, Heidelberg.

Krick, H.
1982: *Das Ritual der Feuergründung*, Wien.

Kripke, S.
1982: *Wittgenstein on Rules and Private Language*, Cambridge, Mass.

Kuiper, F.B.J.
1960: “The Ancient Aryan Verbal Contest”, *Indo-Iranian Journal* 4, 217-281.
1964: “The Bliss of Aša”, *Indo-Iranian Journal* 8, 96-129.
1971: “An Indian Prometheus?”, *Asiatische Studien* 25, 85-98.

Liebert, G.
1949: *Das Nominalsuffix -ti- im Altindischen*, Lund

Lorenz, K.
1963: *Das sogenannte Böse*, Wien

Lüders, H.
1951-1959: *Varuṇa I-II*, Göttingen.

Macdonell, A.A.
1897: *Vedic Mythology*, Strassburg.

Mittwede, M.
1989: *Textkritische Bemerkungen zur Maitrāyaṇīya Saṃhitā*, Stuttgart

Oberlies, Th.
1998-1999: *Die Religion des Ṛgveda*, Wien

Oguibénine, B.
1988: *La Déesse Uṣas*, Louvain-Paris
1994: Review of Staal (1990), *Indo-Iranian Journal* 37, 263-268

Oldenberg, H.
1917: *Die Religion des Veda, Zweite Auflage*, Stuttgart und Berlin.

Renou, L.
1958: *Études sur le vocabulaire du Ṛgveda*, Pondichéry.

Renou, L. & Filliozat, J.
1947: *L'Inde Classique I*, Paris

Rozin, P.
1976: "The Evolution of Intelligence and Access to the Cognitive Unconscious" in J.M. Sprague and A.N.Epstein (eds.) *Progress in Psychobiology and Phsiological Psychology*, New York

Schlerath, B.
1968: "Altindisch asu-, Awestisch ahu- und ähnlich klingende Wörter", *Pratidānam*, The Hague.

Schmidt, H.-P.
1968: *Bṛhaspati und Indra*, Wiesbaden.

Schmithausen, L.
1994: "Zur Textgeschichte der *pañcāgnividyā*", *Wiener Zeitschrift für die Kunde Südasiens 38*, 43-60

Searle, J.
1969: *Speech Acts*, London

Sperber, D.
1975: *Rethinking Symbolism*, Cambridge
1996: *Explaining Culture*, Oxford

Staal, J.F.
1983: *AGNI I-II*, Berkeley
1989: *Rules without Meaning*, New York

1990: *Jouer avec le feu*, Paris

Tambiah, S.J.
1979: "A Performative Approach to Ritual" *Proceedings of the British Academy*, 65, 113-66

Thieme, P.
1949: *Untersuchung zur Wortkunde und Auslegung des Rigveda*, Halle/Saale.
1979: "Über dualische Bezeichnungen von Himmel und Erde im Veda", *Zeitschrift für vergleichende Sprachwissenschaft* 92, 32ff.

Tomasello, M.
1999: *The Cultural Origins of Human Cognition*, Cambridge, MA

Turner, V.
1972: "Symbols in African Ritual" Science, New Series, Vol. 179, 1100-1105

De Vries, L.
1979: "Vaiśvānará-", *Zeitschrift für vergleichende Sprachwissenschaft 93*

Wilden, E.
2000: *Der Kreislauf der Opfergaben im Veda*, Stuttgart

Wittgenstein, L.
1967: *Philosophical Investigations*, Oxford
1979: *Remarks on Frazer's Golden Bough*, Retford

Witzel, M.
1997: "The Development of the Vedic Canon and its Schools: The Social and Political Milieu", *Inside The Texts Beyond The Texts*, Cambridge

Religionswissenschaft: Forschung und Wissenschaft

Karl-Fritz Daiber

Konfuzianische Transformationen

Eine religiöse Tradition in der Moderne Indonesiens, der Philippinen, Vietnams und Südkoreas

Religionswissenschaft: Forschung und Wissenschaft

LIT

Karl-Fritz Daiber
Konfuzianische Transformationen
Eine religiöse Tradition in der Moderne Indonesiens, der Philippinen, Vietnams und Südkoreas

Seit Ende des 19. Jahrhunderts lassen sich erhebliche Veränderungen der Sozialformen des religiösen Konfuzianismus beobachten. Dieser Übergang zur Moderne verläuft höchst verschiedenartig. Während es in Südkorea zur Ausbildung einer religiösen Organisation kommt, die die Restbestände des in staatlichen Akademien institutionalisierten Konfuzianismus verwaltet, entstehen in Vietnam keine neuen Organisationsbildungen. In Indonesien bildet sich unter der chinesischen Minderheit eine konfuzianische Religionsgemeinschaft. Auf den Philippinen bleibt der religiöse Konfuzianismus unter den Chinesen ohne Organisation.

Bd. 9, 2010, 344 S., 34,90 €, br., ISBN 978-3-643-10953-8

LIT Verlag Berlin – Münster – Wien – Zürich – London

Auslieferung Deutschland / Österreich / Schweiz: siehe Impressumsseite